Securing the Internet of Things

Shancang Li

Li Da Xu

Imed Romdhani, Contributor

SYNGRESS

elsevier.com

Syngress is an imprint of Elsevier
50 Hampshire Street, 5th Floor, Cambridge, MA 02139, United States

Copyright © 2017 Elsevier Inc. All rights reserved.

No part of this publication may be reproduced or transmitted in any form or by any means, electronic or mechanical, including photocopying, recording, or any information storage and retrieval system, without permission in writing from the publisher. Details on how to seek permission, further information about the Publisher's permissions policies and our arrangements with organizations such as the Copyright Clearance Center and the Copyright Licensing Agency, can be found at our website: www.elsevier.com/permissions.

This book and the individual contributions contained in it are protected under copyright by the Publisher (other than as may be noted herein).

Notices
Knowledge and best practice in this field are constantly changing. As new research and experience broaden our understanding, changes in research methods, professional practices, or medical treatment may become necessary.

Practitioners and researchers must always rely on their own experience and knowledge in evaluating and using any information, methods, compounds, or experiments described herein. In using such information or methods they should be mindful of their own safety and the safety of others, including parties for whom they have a professional responsibility.

To the fullest extent of the law, neither the Publisher nor the authors, contributors, or editors, assume any liability for any injury and/or damage to persons or property as a matter of products liability, negligence or otherwise, or from any use or operation of any methods, products, instructions, or ideas contained in the material herein.

British Library Cataloguing-in-Publication Data
A catalogue record for this book is available from the British Library

Library of Congress Cataloging-in-Publication Data
A catalog record for this book is available from the Library of Congress

ISBN: 978-0-12-804458-2

For Information on all Syngress publications
visit our website at https://www.elsevier.com

Working together
to grow libraries in
developing countries

www.elsevier.com • www.bookaid.org

Publisher: Todd Green
Acquisition Editor: Brian Romer
Editorial Project Manager: Anna Valutkevich
Production Project Manager: Punithavathy Govindaradjane
Designer: Mark Rogers

Typeset by MPS Limited, Chennai, India

Contents

About the Authors

Shancang Li is a Senior Lecturer in Department of Computer Science and Creative Technologies, University of the West of England, Bristol, UK. Shancang previously worked as a lecturer at Edinburgh Napier University and as security researcher in Cryptographic Group at University of Bristol where he conducted mobile/digital forensics across a range of industries and technologies. His security background ranges from network penetration testing, wireless security, mobile security, and digital forensics.

Li Da Xu is an IEEE Fellow and an academician of Russian Academy of Engineering. He is an Eminent Professor in Department of Information Technology and Decision Science at Old Dominion University, Norfolk, VA, USA. He was recognized as a Highly Cited Researcher in 2016 by Thomson Reuters. According to Thomson Reuters, *"Highly Cited Researchers 2016 represent some of world's most influential scientific minds."*

He is the Founding Chair of IFIP TC8 WG8.9, Founding Chair of the IEEE SMC Society Technical Committee on Enterprise Information Systems, and Founding Editor-in-Chief of the journals titled, *Journal of Industrial Information Integration* (Elsevier BV), *Journal of Industrial Integration and Management* (World Scientific), *Enterprise Information Systems* (Taylor & Francis) and Founding Co-Editor-in-Chief of *Frontiers of Engineering Management* (Higher Education Press) and *Journal of Management Analytics* (Taylor & Francis).

In addition to these notable achievements, he is also an endowed Changjiang Chair Professor in the Ministry of Education of China. Dr. Xu's affiliations include the Institute of Computing Technology, the Chinese Academy of Sciences, the University of Science and Technology of China, Shanghai Jiao Tong University, the China State Council Development Research Center, and Old Dominion University, VA, USA.

He participated in early research and educational academic activities in the subject of systems science and engineering. Professor Xu collaborated and worked extensively with pioneering scholars such as West Churchman, John Warfield, and Qian Xuesen. Furthermore, he spearheaded early research and educational academic activities in the subject of information systems and enterprise systems, which was started in the early 1980s.

Many consider him to be one of the founding fathers of an emerging discipline called Industrial Information Integration Engineering. He is the author of the recent book entitled *Enterprise Integration and Information Architecture* and the coauthor of the book entitled *Systems Science Methodological Approaches* published by Taylor & Francis Group. Many well-known scholars including Qian Xuesen have cited his work in their seminal research.

CHAPTER 1

Introduction: Securing the Internet of Things

Shancang Li

1.1 INTRODUCTION

The emerging Internet of Things (IoT) is believed to be the next generation of the Internet and will become an attractive target for hackers (Roman et al., 2011), in which billions of things are interconnected. Each physical object in the IoT is able to interact without human interventions (Bi et al., 2014). In recent years, a variety of applications with different infrastructures have been developed, such as logistics, manufacturing, healthcare, industrial surveillance, etc. (ITU, 2013; Pretz, 2013). A number of cutting-edge techniques (such as intelligent sensors, wireless communication, networks, data analysis technologies, cloud computing, etc.) have been developed to realize the potential of the IoT with different intelligent systems (Bi et al., 2014; Tan et al., 2014). However, technologies for the IoT are still in their infant stages and a lot of technical difficulties associated with IoT need to be overcomed (Li et al., 2014c). One of the most significant obstacles in IoT is security (Li et al., 2014c), which involves the sensing of infrastructure security, communication network security, application security, and general system security (Keoh et al., 2014). To address the security challenges in IoT, we will analyze the security problems in IoT based on four-layer architecture.

1.1.1 Overview

The concept of IoT was firstly proposed in 1999 (Li et al., 2014c) and the exact definition is still subjective to different perspectives taken (Hepp et al., 2007; ITU, 2013; Li et al., 2014c; Pretz, 2013). The IoT is believed to be the future Internet for the new generation, which integrates various ranges of technologies, including sensory, communication, networking, service-oriented architecture (SoA), and intelligent information processing technologies (Council, 2008; Li et al., 2014c; Lim et al., 2013). However, it also brings a number of significant challenges, such as security, integration of

Securing the Internet of Things. DOI: http://dx.doi.org/10.1016/B978-0-12-804458-2.00001-9
© 2017 Elsevier Inc. All rights reserved.

hybrid networks, intelligent sensing technologies, etc. Security is the chief among them, which plays a fundamental role to protect the IoT against attacks and malfunctions (Roman et al., 2011). Traditionally, the security means cryptography, secure communication, and privacy assurances. However, in IoT security encompasses a wider range of tasks, including data confidentiality, services availability, integrity, antimalware, information integrity, privacy protection, access control, etc. (Keoh et al., 2014).

As an open ecosystem, the IoT security is orthogonal to other research areas. The great diversity of IoT makes it very vulnerable to attacks against availability, service integrity, security, and privacy. At the lower layer of IoT (sensing layer), the sensing devices/technologies have very limited computation capacity and energy supply and cannot provide well security protection; at the middle layers (such as network layer, service layer), the IoT relies on networking and communications which facilitates eavesdropping, interception, and denial of service (DoS) attacks. For example, in network layer, a self-organized topology without centralized control is prone to attacks against authentication, such as node replication, node suppression, node impersonation, etc. At the upper layer (such as application layer), the data aggregation and encryption turn out to be useful to mitigate the scalability and vulnerability problems of all layers. To build a trustworthy IoT, a system-level security analytics and self-adaptive security policy framework are needed.

1.1.2 State-of-the-Art

The IoT is an extension of the Internet by integrating mobile networks, Internet, social networks, and intelligent things to provide better services or applications to users (Cai et al., 2014; Gu et al., 2014; Hoyland et al., 2014; Kang et al., 2014; Keoh et al., 2014; Li et al., 2014a; Li et al., 2014b; Tao et al., 2014; Xiao et al., 2014; Xu et al., 2014a; Xu et al., 2014b; Yuan Jie et al., 2014). The success of IoT depends on the standardization of security at various levels, which provides secured interoperability, compatibility, reliability, and effectiveness of the operations on a global scale (Li et al., 2014c). The importance of IoT has been recognized as top national strategies by many countries. The IoT European Research Cluster sponsored a number of IoT fundamental research projects: IoT-A was launched to design a reference model and architecture for IoT, while the ongoing RERUM project focuses on IoT security (Floerkemeier et al., 2007; Gama et al., 2012; Welbourne et al., 2009). The Japanese government proposed u-Japan and i-Japan strategies to promote a sustainable Information, Communication, and Technology (ICT) society (Ning, 2013). In United States, the information technology and innovation foundation (ITIF) focuses on new information and communication technologies for IoT (He and Xu, 2012; Xu, 2011). The South Korea conducted RFID/USN and "New IT Strategy" program to advance the IoT infrastructure development (Xu, 2011). The China government officially launched the "Sensing China" program in 2010 (Bi et al., 2014).

Technically, a very diverse range of networking and communication technologies is available for IoT, such as WiFi, ZigBee (IEEE 802.15.4), BLE (Low energy Bluetooth), ANT, etc. More specifically, the Internet Engineering Task Force (IETF) has standardized 6LoWPAN (IPv6 over Low-Power Wireless Personal Area Networks), ROLL (routing over low-power and lossy-networks), and CoAP (constrained application protocol) to equip constrained devices (Cai et al., 2014; Chen et al., 2014; Esad-Djou, 2014; Gu et al., 2014; Hoyland et al., 2014; HP Company, 2014; Kang et al., 2014; Keoh et al., 2014; Li and Xiong, 2013; Li et al., 2014a; Oppliger, 2011; Raza et al., 2013; Roe, 2014; Tan et al., 2014; Wang and Wu, 2010; Xiao et al., 2014; Xu et al., 2014a, b; Yao et al., 2013). Concerns over the authenticity of software and protection of intellectual property produced various software verification and attestation techniques often referred to as trusted or measured boot. The confidentiality of data has always been and remains a primary concern. Security control mechanisms have been developed to ensure the security of data transmission in wireless communication and in motion, such as 802.11i (WPA2) or 802.1AE (MACsec). Recently, the security standards for the RFID market have been reported in Raza et al. (2012). For RFID applications, European Commission (EC) has released several recommendations to outline the following security issues in a lawful, ethical, socially, and politically acceptable way (Di Pietro et al., 2014; Esad-Djou, 2014; Furnell, 2007; Gaur, 2013; HP Company, 2014; Raza et al., 2012; Roe, 2014; Roman et al., 2013; Weber, 2013):

- Measuring the deployment of RFID applications to ensure that national legislation is complying with the EU Data Protection Directive 95/46, 99/5, and 2002/58.
- A framework for privacy and data protection impact assessments has been proposed (PIA; No. 4).
- Assessment of implications of the application implementation for the protection of personal data and privacy (No. 5).
- Identifying any applications that might raise information security threats.
- Checking the information.
- Issuing recommendations that concern the privacy information and transparency on RFID use.

But for IoT, the security problem is still a challenging area. Billions of devices might be connected in IoT and well-designed security architecture is needed to fully protect the information and allow data to be securely shared over IoT.

New security challenges will be created by the endless variety of IoT applications. For example:

- Industrial security concerns, including the intelligent sensors, embedded programmable logic controllers (PLCs), robotic systems, which are typically integrated with IoT infrastructure. Security control on the IoT industrial infrastructure is a big concern.
- Hybrid system security controls. The IoT might involve many hybrid systems, how to provide cross-system security protection is crucial for the success of the IoT.
- For the new business processes created in IoT, a security is needed to protect the business information and data.
- IoT end-node security, how the end-nodes receive software updates, or security patches in a timely manner without impairing functional safety is a challenging.

1.1.3 Security Requirements

In IoT, each connected device could be a potential doorway into the IoT infrastructure or personal data (HP Company, 2014; Roe, 2014). The data security and privacy concerns are very important but the potential risks associated with the IoT will reach new levels as interoperability, mashups, and autonomous decision-making begin to embed complexity, security loopholes, and potential vulnerability. Privacy risks will arise in the IoT since the complexity may create more vulnerability that is related to the service. In IoT, much information is related with our personal information, such as date of birth, location, budgets, etc. This is one aspect of the big data challenging, and security professions will need to ensure that they think through the potential privacy risks associated with the entire data set. The IoT should be implemented in a lawful, ethical, socially, and politically acceptable way, where legal challenges, systematic approaches, technical challenges, and business challenges should be considered. This chapter focuses on the technical implementation design of the security IoT architecture. Security must be addressed throughout the IoT lifecycle from the initial design to the services running. The main research challenges in IoT scenario include the data confidentiality, privacy, and trust, as shown in Fig. 1.1 (Di Pietro et al., 2014; Furnell, 2007; Gaur, 2013; Miorandi et al., 2012; Roman et al., 2013; Weber, 2013).

To well illustrate the security requirements in IoT, we modeled the IoT as four-layer architecture: *sensing layer*, *network layer*, *service layer*, and *application—interface layer*. Each layer is able to provide corresponding security controls, such as access control, device authentication, data integrity and confidentiality in transmission, availability, and the ability of

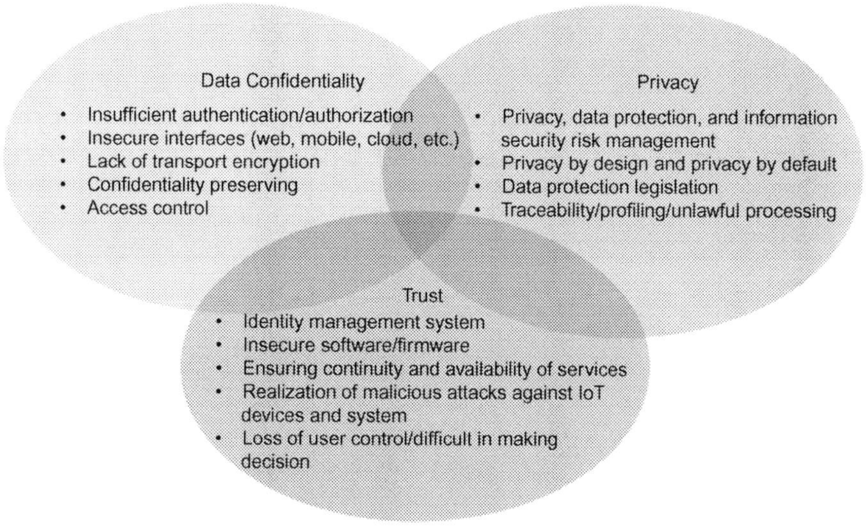

Data Confidentiality
- Insufficient authentication/authorization
- Insecure interfaces (web, mobile, cloud, etc.)
- Lack of transport encryption
- Confidentiality preserving
- Access control

Privacy
- Privacy, data protection, and information security risk management
- Privacy by design and privacy by default
- Data protection legislation
- Traceability/profiling/unlawful processing

Trust
- Identity management system
- Insecure software/firmware
- Ensuring continuity and availability of services
- Realization of malicious attacks against IoT devices and system
- Loss of user control/difficult in making decision

FIGURE 1.1

Security issues in IoT.

Table 1.1 Top Ten Vulnerabilities in IoT

Security Concerns	Interface Layer	Service Layer	Network Layer	Sensing Layer
Insecure web interface	√	√	√	
Insufficient authentication/ authorization	√	√	√	√
Insecure network services		√	√	
Lack of transport encryption		√	√	
Privacy concerns		√	√	√
Insecure Cloud interface	√			
Insecure mobile interface	√		√	√
Insecure security configuration	√	√	√	
Insecure software/firmware	√		√	
Poor physical security			√	√

antivirus or attacks. In Table 1.1, the most important security concerns in IoT are summarized.

The security requirements depend on each of these particularly sensing technology, networks, layers, and have been identified in the following sections.

1.2   SECURITY REQUIREMENTS IN IoT ARCHITECTURE

A critical requirement of IoT is that the devices must be interconnected, which makes it be able to perform specific tasks, such as sensing, communicating, information processing, etc. The IoT is able to acquire, transmit, and process the information from the IoT end-nodes (such as RFID devices, sensors, gateway, intelligent devices, etc.) via network to accomplish highly complex tasks. The IoT should be able to provide applications with strong security protection (e.g., for online payment application, the IoT should be able to protect the integrity of payment information).

The system architecture must provide operational guarantees for the IoT, which bridges the gap between the physical devices and the virtual worlds. In designing the framework of IoT, following factors should be taken into consideration: (1) technical factors, such as sensing techniques, communication methods, network technologies, etc.; (2) security protection, such as information confidentiality, transmission security, privacy protection, etc.; (3) business issues, such as business models, business processes, etc. Currently, the SoA has been successfully applied to IoT design, where the applications are moving towards service-oriented integration technologies. In business domain, the complex applications among diverse services have been appearing. Services reside in different layers of the IoT such as: sensing layer, network layer, services layer, and application—interface layer. The services-based application will heavily depend on the architecture of IoT. Fig. 1.2 depicts a generic SoA for IoT, which consists of four layers:

- *Sensing layer* is integrated with end components of IoT to sense and acquire the information of devices;

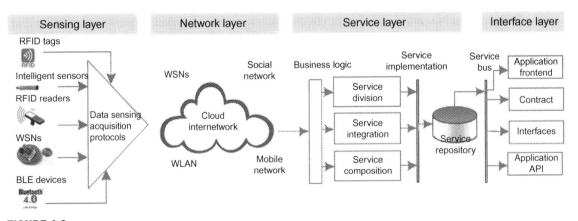

FIGURE 1.2
SoA for IoT (Bi et al., 2014).

- *Network layer* is the infrastructure to support wireless or wired connections among things;
- *Service layer* is to provide and manage services required by users or applications;
- *Application–interfaces layer* consists of interaction methods with users or applications.

The security requirements on each layer might be different due to its features. In general, the security solution for the IoT considers following requirements: (1) sensing layer and IoT end-node security requirements, (2) network layer security requirements, (3) service layer security requirements, (4) application–interface layer security requirements, (5) the security requirements between layers, and (6) security requirements for services running and maintenance.

1.2.1 Sensing Layer and IoT End-Nodes

The IoT is a multilayer network that interconnects devices for information acquisition, exchange, and processing. At the sensing layer, the intelligent tags and sensor networks are able to automatically sense the environment and exchange data among devices (Li et al., 2014c). In determining the sensing layer of an IoT, the main concerns are:

- *Cost, size, resource,* and *energy consumption.* The things might be equipped with sensing devices such as RFID tags, sensors, actuator, etc., which should be designed to minimize required resources as well as cost.
- *Deployment.* The IoT end-nodes (such as RFID reader, tags, sensors, etc.) can be deployed one-time, or in incremental or random ways depending on application requirements.
- *Heterogeneity.* A variety of things or hybrid networks make the IoT very heterogeneous.
- *Communication.* The IoT end-nodes should be designed in such a way that it is able to communicate with each other.
- *Networks.* The IoT involves hybrid networks, such as Wireless Sensor Networks (WSNs), WMNs, and supervisory control and data acquisition (SCADA) systems.

The security is an important concern in sensing layer. It is expected that IoT could be connected with industrial networks to provide users with smart services. However, it may cause new concerns in devices controlling, such as who can input authentication credentials or decide whether an application should be trusted. The security model in IoT must be able to make its own judgments and decision about whether to accept a command or execute a task. At sensing layer, the devices are designed for low power consumption with constraints resources, which often have limited connectivity. The endless variety of IoT applications poses an equally wide variety of security challenges.

- Devices authentication
- Trusted devices
- Leveraging the security controls and availability of infrastructures in sensing layer.
- In terms of software update, how the sensing devices receive software updates or security patches in a timely manner without impairing functional safety or incurring significant recertification costs every time a patch is rolled out.

In this layer, the security concerns can be classified into two main categories:

- The security requirements at IoT end-node: physically security protection, access control, authentication, nonrepudiation, confidentiality, integrity, availability, and privacy.
- The security requirements in sensing layer: confidentiality, data source authentication, device authentication, integrity, availability, and timeless.

Table 1.2 summarizes the potential security threats and security vulnerabilities at IoT end-node and Table 1.3 analyses the security threats and vulnerabilities in sensing layer.

To secure devices in this layer before users are at risk, following actions should be taken: (1) Implement security standards for IoT and ensure all

Table 1.2 Security Threats and Vulnerabilities at IoT End-Node

Security Threats	Description
Unauthorized access	Due to physically capture or logic attacked, the sensitive information at the end-nodes is captured by the attacker
Availability	The end-node stops to work since physically captured or attacked logically
Spoofing attack	With malware node, the attacker successfully masquerades as IoT end-device, end-node, or end-gateway by falsifying data
Selfish threat	Some IoT end-nodes stop working to save resources or bandwidth to cause the failure of network
Malicious code	Virus, Trojan, and junk message that can cause software failure
DoS	An attempt to make a IoT end-node resource unavailable to its users
Transmission threats	Threats in transmission, such as interrupting, blocking, data manipulation, forgery, etc.
Routing attack	Attacks on a routing path

Table 1.3 Analysis of the Security Threats and Vulnerabilities in Sensing Layer

IoT End-Node Threats and Vulnerabilities	IoT End-Devices	IoT End-Node	IoT End-Gateway
Unauthorized access	√	√	√
Selfish threat		√	√
Spoofing attack		√	√
Malicious code	√	√	√
DoS	√	√	√
Transmission threats			√
Routing attack	√	√	√

devices are produced by meeting specific security standards; (2) Build trustworthy data sensing system and review the security of all devices/components; (3) Forensically identify and trace the source of users; (4) Software or firmware at IoT end-node should be securely designed.

1.2.2 Network Layer

The network layer connects all things in IoT and allows them to be aware of their surroundings. It is capable of aggregating data from existing IT infrastructures and then transmitted to other layers, such as sensing layer, service layers, etc. The IoT connects a variety of different networks, which may cause a lot of difficulties on network problems, security problems, and communication problems.

The deployment, management, and scheduling of networks are essential for the network layer in IoT. This enables devices to perform tasks collaboratively. In the networking layer, the following issues should be addressed:

- Network management technologies including the management for fixed, wireless, mobile networks,
- Network energy efficiency,
- Requirements of QoS,
- Technologies for mining and searching,
- Information confidentiality,
- Security and privacy.

Among these issues, information confidentiality and human privacy and security are critical because of its deployment, mobility, and complexity. The existing network security technologies can provide a basis for privacy and security protection in IoT, but more works still need to be done. The security requirements in network layer involve:

- *Overall security requirements*, including confidentiality, integrity, privacy protection, authentication, group authentication, keys protection, availability, etc.
- *Privacy leakage*: Since some IoT devices physically located in untrusted places, which cause potential risks for attackers to physically find the privacy information such as user identification, etc.
- *Communication security*: It involves the integrity and confidentiality of signaling in IoT communications.
- *Overconnected*: The overconnected IoT may run risk of losing control of the user. Two security concerns may be caused: (1) DoS attack, the bandwidth required by signaling authentication can cause network congestion and further cause DoS; (2) Keys security, for the overconnected network, the keys operations could cause heavy network resources consumption.
- *MITM attack*: The attacker makes independent connections with the victims and relays messages between them, making them believe that they are talking directly to each other over a private connection, when in fact the attacker controls the entire conversation.
- *Fake network message*: Attackers could create fake signaling to isolate/misoperate the devices from the IoT.

In the network layer, the possible security threats are summarized in Table 1.4 and in Table 1.5 the potential security threats and vulnerabilities are analyzed.

The network infrastructure and protocols developed for IoT are different with existing IP network, special efforts are needed on following security concerns: (1) Authentication/Authorization, which involves vulnerabilities such as

Table 1.4 Security Threats in Network Layer

Security Threats	Description
Data breach	Information released of secure information to an untrusted environment
Public key and private key	It comprises of keys in networks
Malicious code	Virus, Trojan, and junk message that can cause software failure
DoS	An attempt to make an IoT end-node resource unavailable to its users
Transmission threats	Threats in transmission, such as interrupting, blocking, data manipulation, forgery, etc.
Routing attack	Attacks on a routing path

	Privacy Leakage	Confidentiality	Integrity	DoS	PKI	MITM	Request Forgery
Physical protection	√	√					√
Transmission security		√	√	√	√	√	√
Overconnected			√	√	√		
Cross-layer fusion	√	√				√	√

Table 1.5 The Security Threats and Vulnerabilities in Network Layer

password, access control, etc. and (2) Secure transport encryption—it is crucial to encrypt the transmission in this layer.

1.2.3 Service Layer

In IoT, the service layer relies on middleware technology, which is an important enabler of services and applications. The service layer provides IoT a cost-effective platform where the hardware and software platforms could be reused. The IoT illustrates the activities required by the middle service specifications, which are undertaken by various standards developed by the service providers and organizations. The service layer is designed based on the common requirements of applications, application programming interfaces (APIs), and service protocols. The core set of services in this layer might include following components: event processing service, integration services, analytics services, UI services, and security and management services (Choi et al., 2012). The activities in service layer, such as information exchange, data processing, ontologies databases, communications between services, are conducted by following components:

- *Service discovery*. It finds infrastructure that can provide the required service and information in an effective way.
- *Service composition*. It enables the combination and interaction among the connected things. Discovery exploits the relationships of things to find the desired service, and service composition schedules or recreates more suitable services to obtain the most reliable ones.
- *Trustworthiness management*. It aims to understand the trusted devices and information provided by other services.
- *Service APIs*. It provides the interactions between services required by users.

Recently, a number of service layer solutions have been reported. The SOCRADES integration architecture is proposed that can be used to interact between applications and service layers effectively (Fielding and Taylor, 2002);

things are abstracted as devices to provide services at low levels as network discovery services, metadata exchange services, and asynchronous publish and subscribe event (Kranenburg et al., 2011; Sundmaeker et al., 2010); In Peris-Lopez et al. (2006), a representational state transfer is defined to increase interoperability between loosely coupled services and distributed applications. In Hernandez-Castro et al. (2013), the services layer introduced a service provisioning process that can provide the interaction between applications and services. It is important to design an effective security strategy to protect services against attacks in the service layer. The security requirements in the service layer include:

- Authorization, service authentication, group authentication, privacy protection, integrity, security of keys, nonrepudiation, antireplay, availability, etc.
- Privacy leakage. The main concern in this layer involves privacy leakage and malicious location tracking.
- Service abuses. In IoT the service abuse attack involves: (i) illegal abuse of services; (ii) abuse of unsubscribed services.
- Node identify masquerade.
- DoS attack.
- Replay attack, the attacker resends the data.
- Service information sniffer and manipulation.
- Repudiation in service layer, it includes the communication repudiation and services repudiation.

The security solution should be able to protect the operations on this layer from potential threats. Table 1.6 summarizes the security threats on the service layer.

Table 1.6 The Security Threats in Service Layer

Security Threats	Description
Privacy threats	Privacy leakage or malicious location tracking
Services abuse	Unauthorized user access services or the authorized users access unsubscribed services
Identity masquerade	The IoT end-device, node, or gateway are masqueraded by attacker
Service information manipulation	The information in services is manipulated by the attacker
Repudiation	Denial of the operations have been done
DoS	An attempt to make an IoT end-node resource unavailable to its users
Replay attack	The attack resends the information to spoof the receiver
Routing attack	Attacks on a routing path

Ensure the data in service layer security is crucial but it is difficult. It involves fragmented, full of competing standards, and proprietary solutions. The SoA is very helpful to improve the security of this layer, but following challenges still need to be faced when building an IoT services or application: (1) data transmission security between service and/or layers; (2) secure services management, such as service identification, access control, services composite, etc.

1.2.4 Application–Interface Layer

The application–interface layer involves a variety of applications and interfaces from RFID tag tracking to smart home, which are implemented by standard protocols as well as service-composition technologies (Ning et al., 2013). The requirements in application–interface layer strongly depend on the applications. For the application maintenance, following security requirements will be involved:

- Remote safe configuration, software downloading and updating, security patches, administrator authentication, unified security platform, etc.
    For the security requirements on communications between layers:
- Integrity and confidentiality for transmission between layers, cross-layer authentication and authorization, sensitive information isolation, etc.

In IoT in designing the security solutions, following rules should be helpful:

a. Since most constrained IoT end-nodes work in an unattended manner, the designer should pay more attention to the safety of these nodes;
b. As IoT involves billions of clustering nodes, the security solutions should be designed based on energy efficiency schemes;
c. The light security scheme at IoT end-nodes might be different with existing network security solutions; however, we should design security solutions in a big enough range for all parts in IoT.

Table 1.7 summarizes the security threats and vulnerabilities in IoT application–interface layer.

Table 1.7 The Security Threats in Application–Interface Layer

Security Threats	Description
Remote configuration	Fail to configure at interfaces
Misconfiguration	Misconfiguration at remote IoT end-node, end-device, or end-gateway
Security management	Log and keys leakage
Management system	Failure of management system

Table 1.8 The Security Threats and Vulnerabilities in Application–Interface Layer

	Unauthorized Access	Failure of Node	Masquerade	Selfish Node	Trojan, Virus, Spam	Privacy Leakage
Physically security protection	✓	✓	✓			
Antivirus, firewalling				✓		
Access control	✓	✓	✓			✓
Confidential	✓	✓	✓			✓
Data integrity		✓	✓	✓	✓	
Availability						
Authentication	✓	✓	✓			✓
Nonrepudiation	✓	✓	✓			✓

Table 1.9 Security Threats Between Layers in the IoT Architecture

Security Threats	Description
Sensitive information leakage at border	The sensitive information might be not protected at the border of layers
Identity spoofing	The identities in different layers have different priorities
Sensitive information spreads between layers	Sensitive information spreads at different layers and causes information leakage

In Table 1.8, we analyze the security threats and potential vulnerabilities in application–interface layer.

The application–interface layer bridges the IoT system with user applications, which should be able to ensure that the interaction of IoT systems with other applications or users are legal and can be trusted.

1.2.5   Cross-Layer Threats

Information in the IoT architecture might be shared among all of the four layers to achieve full interoperability between services and devices. It brings a number of security challenges such as trust guarantee, privacy of the users, and their date, secure data sharing among layers, etc. In the IoT architecture described in Fig. 1.2, information is exchanged between different layers, which may cause potential threats as shown in Table 1.9.

The security requirements in this layer include (1) security protection, securing to be ensured at design and execution time; (2) privacy protection, personal information access within IoT system, privacy standards, and enhancement technologies; (3) trust has to be a part of IoT architecture and must be built in.

Table 1.10 Security Threats Between Layers in the IoT Architecture

Security Threats	Description
Remote configuration	Fail to configure remote IoT end-node, end-device, or end-gateway
Misconfiguration	Misconfiguration at remote IoT end-node, end-device, or end-gateway
Security management	Log and keys leakage at IoT end-node
Management system	Failure of management system

1.2.6   Threats Caused in Maintenance of IoT

The maintenance of IoT can cause security problems, such as in configuration of the network, security management, and application managements. Table 1.10 summarized the potential threats that can cause risk in IoT.

1.3   SECURITY IN ENABLING TECHNOLOGIES

1.3.1   Security in Identification and Tracking Technologies

The concept of IoT was coined based on the RFID-enabled identification and tracking technologies. A basic RFID system consists of an RFID reader and RFID tags. Due to its capability for identifying, tracing, and tracking, the RFID system has been widely applied in logistics, such as package tracking, supply chain management, healthcare applications, etc. An RFID system could provide sufficient real-time information about things in IoT, which are very useful to manufacturers, distributors, and retailers. For example, RFID application in supply chain management can improve backroom inventory-management practices.

Although RFID technology is successfully used in many areas, it is still evolving in developing active system, Inkjet-printing based RFID, and management technologies (Hepp et al., 2007). For adoption by the IoT, more identified problems need to be resolved, such as: *collision of RFID readings, signal interferences, privacy protection, standardization, integration, etc.*

In the new era of IoT, the scope of identification has expended and included RFIDs, barcodes, and other intelligent sensing technologies. In RFID-enabled contactless technologies (ISO 14443 and 15693), security features have been implemented, such as cryptographic challenge-response authentication, 128-bit AES, triple-DES, and SHA-2 algorithms. The increasing use of RFID devices requires the RFID security guarantee from multiple sides: manufacture,

Table 1.11 Security Features in RFID Standards

Security RFID	Confidentiality	Integrity	Availability
EPC Class 0/0+		✓	✓
EPC Class 1 G1		✓	✓
EPC Class 1 G2	✓	✓	✓
ISO/IEC 18000-2	✓	✓	
ISO/IEC 18000-3	✓	✓	✓
ISO/IEC 11784/5	✓	✓	
ISO/IEC 15693	✓	✓	✓
Nonrepudiation	✓	✓	✓

privacy protection, business processes. In general the security features of RFID include:

- Tags/Readers collision problem
- Data confidentiality
- Tag-to-reader authentication
- High-assurance readers

Table 1.11 summarizes the security features of RFID standards.

In RFID technologies, the security and privacy protection are not just technical issues; important policy questions arise as RFID tags join to create large sensor networks.

1.3.2   Security in Integration of WSN and RFID

The integration of wireless sensors and RFID empowers IoT in the implementation of industrial services and the further deployment of services in extended applications. IoT with the integration of RIFD and WSNs makes it possible to develop IoT applications for healthcare, decision-making of complex systems, and smart civic systems such as smart transport, cities or water supply systems.

The security issue in integration of RFID and WSNs involves following challenges:

- *Privacy*, it involves the privacy of RFID devices and WSNs devices;
- Identification and authentication, the identification has to be protected from tracking by unauthorized user in the network;
- *Communication security*, the communication between RFID devices and IoT devices poses security threats that need to be addressed proactively, and appropriate measures must be implemented well;

- *Trust and ownership*, trust implies the authenticity and integrity of the communication parts such as sensor nodes and RFID tags;
- *Integration*;
- *User authentication*.

1.3.3   Security in Communications

In IoT things are connected together in network access layer through different communication technologies. The IoT can be seen as an aggregation of heterogeneous networks, such as WSNs, wireless mesh networks, mobile networks, RFID systems, and WLAN. The communications between things/networks are essential to make reliable information exchange, which requires the IoT to provide secure, reliable, and scalable connections. IoT would also greatly benefit from the existing communication protocols in Internet such as IPv6, as this addresses any number of things needed through the Internet directly (Pretz, 2013). The basic principles of secure communications in IoT include: *authentication, availability, confidentiality*, and *integrity*. The limit of resources of things makes it difficult to build a secure enough communication for IoT; however, the IoT communication systems have to be designed to provide "secure enough" by finding the right balance between effort and benefit of protection measures. The security solution for communications should be designed high enough so that it will force the hackers to give up before they succeed. The commonly used communication protocols and the potential security features include:

- RFID (e.g., ISO 18000 6c EPC class 1 Gen2), the security features include confidentiality, integrity, and availability. The security features for different standards can be found in Table 1.10.
- NFC, IEEE 802.11 (WLAN), IEEE 802.15.4, IEEE 802.15.1 (Bluetooth), in these wireless communication technologies, following security are needed: confidentiality, integrity, authentication, availability, and detection of malicious intrusion.
- IETF 6LoWPAN. Since 6LoWPAN is a combination of IEEE 802.15.4 and IPv6, which may cause potential vulnerabilities from the two sides that target all layers of the stack (Table 1.12).
- Machine-to-Machine (M2M), tradition disruptive attacks in M2M such as DoS could have new consequences in M2M.
- Traditional IP technologies, such as IP, IPv6, IPv4, etc., secure every device, address nearing exhaustion, networks simply won't have enough addresses to assign to the explosion of devices unless they transit to IPv6. However, for IPv6 it could have further vulnerabilities that haven't been discovered. In IPv6, IPsec could provide authenticity and integrity with authentication header, and the Encapsulated security payload provides

Table 1.12 Security Features in 6LoWPAN

Layers	Main Potential Attacks
Application layer	Overwhelm attack, path-based DoS attack
Transport layer	Flooding attack
Network layer	Malicious node attack; Sybil attack; Wormhole attack, Spoofing attack; routing attack, etc.
Adaption layer	Packets fragmentation attack
Link layer	Exhaustion attack, collision attack, interrogation attack
Physical layer	Tampering attack, etc.

confidentiality. Recently, the transport layer security is developed as an alternative to IPsec to provide mutual authentication of two parties using public key infrastructures and X.509 certificates (Tao et al., 2014).

■ Key Management in IoT. Many key management systems (KMSs) have been proposed recently. In IoT, the KMS should be designed based on standard protocols. The IPsec applies the Internet Key Exchange (IKE) for automatic key management. For IEEE 802.15.4, no KMS is defined but in Cai et al. (2014), a lightweight key management IKEv2 is proposed for 6LoWPAN IPsec and IEEE 802.15.4.

1.3.4   Security in Networks

The IoT is a hybrid network that involves a lot of heterogeneous networks, which requires multifaceted security solutions against network intrusions and disruptions. The IoT contains networks that connect with daily-used devices, such as smartphones, surveillance cameras, home appliances, etc. Support for heterogeneous networks can help IoT to connect the devices with different communication specification, QoS requirements, functionalities, and goals. On the other hand, support for heterogeneity can reduce the cost to implement IoT by well integrating diversified things. Meanwhile, some of the existing networking technologies, such as architecture, protocols, network management, security schemes, can be directly applicable in an IoT context. The networks involved in IoT are core parts of security working, and each subnetwork is required to provide confidentiality, secure communication, encryption certificates, and that sort of things. In IoT no Intrusion Detection System (IDS) and Intrusion Prevention System (IPS) are specifically designed yet, but many watchdog-based IDS and IPSs could be used in the context of IoT.

1.3.5   Security in Service Management

Service management refers to the implementation and management of the services that meet the needs of users or applications. Security solution at service layer is designed specifically in the context of the services. For services such as consumer applications, logistical, surveillance, intelligent healthcare, the security concerns have some similarities: authentication, access control, privacy, integrity of information, certificates and PKI certificates, digital signature and nonrepudiation, etc. For different services, the security concerns might be specifically designed depending on the service feature, scenarios, and special requirements.

1.4 SECURITY CONCERNS IN IoT APPLICATIONS

The IoT enables information gathering, transmitting, and storing to be available for devices in many scenarios, which creates or accelerates many applications such as industrial control systems, retailing industry, smart shelf operations, healthcare, food and restaurant industry, logistic industry, travel and tourism industry, library applications, etc. It can also be foreseen that the IoT will greatly contribute to address the important issues such as business model, healthcare monitoring systems, daily living monitoring, and traffic congestion control.

For applications in IoT, security and privacy are two important challenges. To integrate the devices of sensing layer as intrinsic parts of the IoT, effective security technology is essential to ensure security and privacy protection in various activities such as personal activities, business processes, transportations, and information protection. In this section, we will focus on following five typical applications to address the potential security challenges.

1.4.1 Security Concerns in SCADA Systems

SCADA systems are generally designed as more technical-oriented solutions often in the industrial environment with the sole intent to monitor processes without considering the security requirements and the needs to protect them from external threats. The SCADA systems are believed to play a huge role in industrial applications of IoT (Di Pietro et al., 2014). A SCADA could contain multiple elements: supervisory systems, PLCs, human–machine interface, remote machine telemetry units, communication infrastructure, and various process and analytical instrumentation. From a security viewpoint, an attacker could target each of the above elements to compromise a SCADA system. In order to ensure the integration of SCADA systems into IoT, secure SCADA protocols should be designed to be able to connect with IoT environments. However, this could raise the following security concerns (Bamforth, 2014; Kim, 2012; Perna, 2013):

- *Authentication and access control*. To ensure secure communication, strong authentication must be implemented to allow access to main functionalities. On the other hand, authenticating and access control can well identify and assess the information sources.

- *Identification of SCADA vulnerabilities.* It is important to implement proper countermeasures and take corrective actions as appropriate. The software in SCADA should be regularly updated to tackle the security vulnerabilities.
- *Physical security.* In SCADAs, physical security protection must be carefully evaluated for each component and each component is recommended to meet NIST FIPS standards.
- *System recovery and backups.* The SCADAs should be designed to be able to rapidly recover from disaster or compromised status.

1.4.2   Security Concerns in Enterprise Information Systems

Most companies have fulfilled their missions of installing enterprise information systems within their companies in the last two decades. These enterprise information systems have played the pivotal role in modern organizations existing as Enterprise Resource Planning (ERP) systems which integrated intraorganizational business processes to supply chain management systems that link interorganizational business processes, and Customer Relationship Management (CRM) systems that maintain relationships with customers (Li, 2011). Although the direct financial benefits and business performance of enterprise systems usage are still in controversy according to a series of studies conducted to investigate the enterprise system usage and organizational performance (Hendricks et al., 2007; Hitt et al., 2002; Wieder et al., 2006), most of them reported that enterprise systems usage causes positive impact on organizational operations by improving decision-making processes, and most importantly, integrating information and resources of an organization into one system. Centralizing information and resources is thus identified as the most important factor for adopting enterprise systems. Looking back historically, it is technology innovation that moves the enterprise system's wave forward. The increasing processing power of servers and PCs in the last two decades has enabled the client/server architecture for enterprise systems. It could be foreseen that the increased processing power will shift to small embedded-devices such as RFID tags, which could be widely implemented in many physical objects, leading to the new type of IoT-enabled enterprise systems. The new IoT-enabled enterprise systems extend the current systems and could gather more integrated data and information, bringing the security challenges to a new level. As most enterprise systems are installed inside organizations' intranets, the traditional security issues for enterprise systems mainly involve the identification process for users to access the system (Wieder et al., 2006). However, the IoT-enabled enterprise systems incorporate sensors into the enterprise systems and will involve more security challenges than the traditional enterprise systems because the data and information carried by the sensors might go beyond the enterprise system physically. For example, the collaborative warehouse implemented with the IoT technology gather data from the warehouse outside the ERP system and communicates with the ERP systems through different protocols (Wang et al., 2013). This new architecture of enterprise systems require the security concerns to focus more on the sensor layer as well as the middleware layer because in both there might be issues of data breach at these layers. For the application layer where the IoT applications might interact with the enterprise systems, special attention shall be given to identity authentication and application architecture because this layer is more vulnerable than other layers.

1.4.3   Security Concerns in Social IoT

Social IoT is the spread and diffusion of IoT applications into societal level. Similarly to the socialization of many other technologies, IoT played an important role at the societal level. It will influence every part of our life from entertainment to energy usage. For example, wearable devices such as Google glasses will be very popular in the foreseeable future and the popular UP wristband by Jawbone has proven how popular the wearable devices could be. Other applications such as smart TV, smart meter, and smart home devices all implying a new digital world enabled by IoT are coming. IoT will make our worlds more connected as the connected car and many other connected devices are on the road (Atzori et al., 2012). However, IoT technology alone won't be able to fulfill the task rather, other technologies have to be considered together to function as an integrated process. Social media and mobile APPs all played key role in this socialization of IoT part. In the future, we could see us all connected through social networks and social IoT devices. Security would be an essential part for the social IoT. As we are entering a new digital world enabled by the IoT, security issues in this digital world are a new challenge compared to the previous Internet security. Previous Internet security mainly focuses on the security protocols, antivirus software implementation, and firewalls. The social IoT security shall have some similarity to the Internet security in that they both shall have the security protocols but the social IoT security might involve more complex issues because the social IoT needs to integrate the heterogynous devices together. How to manage the interactions among all these heterogynous devices becomes the top issue for the social IoT security. Data and information communicated over the IoT network need to be managed through a reliable framework. Ethical issues such as privacy, data access right, the degree of openness of data will all influence how the security architecture for social IoT to be constructed. When more and more devices are connected together, the traffic of data over the social IoT will also become a big issue. How to effectively design the traffic so that data over social IoT could be transferred securely in a reliable way will also become challenging.

1.4.4   Confidentiality and Security for IoT-Based Healthcare

The IoT motives *eHealthcare* and mobile healthcare integrated into IoT-based Healthcare, which covers traditional Internet-enabled healthcare applications (such as e-Pharmacy, e-Care, mobile healthcare, etc.). Similar to the social IoT security, the healthcare IoT security will involve integration of multisource data and information distributed over both the Internet and evolving IoT. As the healthcare is a highly sensitive yet personal area dealing with much private information from patients, especially the vulnerable group of people, the security design shall be paid more attention than many other IoT networks. For this reason, data confidentiality and data security might emerge as the most important factors to be considered when designing the healthcare security architecture. Other factors such as reliability (antihacker, antivirus, etc.), design issues (such as signature, authentication, etc.), and compliance issues shall also be carefully considered. In addition to the previous factors, healthcare security is different from other industries, which features:

- Not bilateral condition;
- Regulated;
- Community interested;
- Legal issues.

For these reasons, the design of the healthcare security system shall adopt a more reliable approach. The current healthcare-specific security standards include following four parts:

- Authentication, identification, signature, nonrepudiation;
- Data integrity, encryption, data integrity process, permanence;
- System security, communication, processing, storage, permanence;
- Internet security, personal health records, secures Internet services.

In IoT-based healthcare system, the security issues include:

- Security for patient confidentiality,
- Security that enables electronic health records (authentication, data integrity),
- Transmission security,
- Security in healthcare data access, processing, storage, etc.

1.5   SUMMARY

Security at both the physical devices and service applications is critical to the operation of IoT, which is indispensable for the success of IoT. Open problems remain in a number of areas, such as security and privacy protection, network protocols, standardization, identity management, trusted architecture, etc. In this chapter, we analyzed the security requirements and potential threats in a four-layer architecture, in terms of general devices security, communication security, network security, and application security. The security challenges in enabling technologies of IoT also are reviewed. In future research, the security strategies for IoT should be carefully designed by managing the tradeoffs among security, privacy, and utility to provide security in multilayer architecture of IoT.

References

Atzori, L., Iera, A., Morabito, G., Nitti, M., 2012. The social internet of things (siot)—when social networks meet the internet of things: concept, architecture and network characterization. Comput. Networks 56 (16), 3594—3608.

Bamforth, R., 2014. Internet of things, scada, ipv6 and social networking.

Bi, Z., Xu, L., Wang, C., 2014. Internet of things for enterprise systems of modern manufacturing. IEEE Transact. Indust. Informat.

Cai, H., Xu, L., Xu, B., Xie, C., Qin, S., Jiang, L., 2014. IoT-based configurable information service platform for product lifecycle management.

Chen, Y., Han, F., Yang, Y.-H., Ma, H., Han, Y., Jiang, C., et al., 2014. Time-reversal wireless paradigm for green internet of things: an overview.

Choi, J., Li, S., Wang, X., Ha, J., 2012. A general distributed consensus algorithm for wireless sensor networks. Paper presented at the Wireless Advanced (WiAd), 2012.

Council, N., 2008. Disruptive civil technologies: six technologies with potential impacts on us interests out to 2025. Paper presented at the Conference Report CR.

Di Pietro, R., Guarino, S., Verde, N., Domingo-Ferrer, J., 2014. Security in wireless ad-hoc networks—a survey. Comput. Commun. 51, 1—20.

Esad-Djou, M., 2014. IT-security: Weblogic server and oracle platform security services (OPSS). Retrieved from <http://thecattlecrew.wordpress.com/2014/02/17/it-security-weblogic-server_1/>.

Fielding, R.T., Taylor, R.N., 2002. Principled design of the modern web architecture. ACM Transact. Internet Technol. 2 (2), 115—150.

Floerkemeier, C., Roduner, C., Lampe, M., 2007. RFID application development with the accada middleware platform. IEEE Syst. J. 1 (2), 82—94.

Furnell, S., 2007. Making security usable: Are things improving? Comput. Security 26 (6), 434—443.

Gama, K., Touseau, L., Donsez, D., 2012. Combining heterogeneous service technologies for building an internet of things middleware. Comput. Commun. 35 (4), 405—417.

Gaur, H., 2013. Internet of things: thinking services.

Gu, L., Wang, J., Sun, B., 2014. Trust management mechanism for internet of things. China Commun. 11 (2), 148—156.

He, W., Xu, L., 2012. Integration of distributed enterprise applications: a survey.

Hendricks, K.B., Singhal, V.R., Stratman, J.K., 2007. The impact of enterprise systems on corporate performance: a study of ERP, SCM, and CRM system implementations. J. Operat. Manage. 25 (1), 65—82.

Hepp, M., Siorpaes, K., Bachlechner, D., 2007. Harvesting wiki consensus: using Wikipedia entries as vocabulary for knowledge management. IEEE Internet Comput. 11 (5), 54−65.

Hernandez-Castro, J.C., Tapiador, J.M.E., Peris-Lopez, P., Li, T., Quisquater, J.-J., 2013. Cryptanalysis of the SASI ultra-light weight RFID authentication protocol. arxiv.

Hitt, L.M., Wu, D., Zhou, X., 2002. Investment in enterprise resource planning: business impact and productivity measures. J. Manage. Informat. Syst. 19 (1), 71−98.

Hoyland, C.A.M., Adams, K., Tolk, A., Xu, L.D., 2014. The rq-tech methodology: a new paradigm for conceptualizing strategic enterprise architectures. J. Manage. Analyt. 1 (1), 55−77.

HP Company, 2014. Internet of things research study. Retrieved from <http://h30499.www3.hp.com/hpeb/attachments/hpeb/application-security-fortify-on-demand/189/1/HP_IoT_Research_Study.pdf>.

ITU, 2013. The internet of things, international telecommunication union (ITU) internet report.

Kang, K., Pang, Z., Da Xu, L., Ma, L., Wang, C., 2014. An interactive trust model for application market of the internet of things. IEEE Trans. Indust. Informat. 10 (2), 1516−1526.

Keoh, S., Kumar, S., Tschofenig, H., 2014. Securing the internet of things: a standardization perspective.

Kim, H., 2012. Security and vulnerability of SCADA systems over ip-based wireless sensor networks. Int. J. Distrib. Sensor Networks 2012, 1−10.

Kranenburg, R.V., Anzelmo, E., Bassi, A., Caprio, D., Dodson, S., Ratto, M., 2011. The internet of things. Paper presented at the 1st Berlin Symposium on Internet and Society (Versión electrónica). Consultado el.

Li, D.X., 2011. Enterprise systems: state-of-the-art and future trends. IEEE Transact. Indust. Informat. 7 (4), 630−640.

Li, F., Xiong, P., 2013. Practical secure communication for integrating wireless sensor networks into the internet of things.

Li, L., Li, S., Zhao, S., 2014a. Qos-aware scheduling of services-oriented internet of things.

Li, L., Wang, B., Wang, A., 2014b. An emergency resource allocation model for maritime chemical spill accidents. J. Manage. Analyt. 1, 146−155.

Li, S., Xu, L.D., Zhao, S., 2014c. The internet of things: a survey. Informat. Syst. Front. 17, 243−259.

Lim, M.K., Bahr, W., Leung, S.C., 2013. Rfid in the warehouse: a literature analysis (1995−2010) of its applications, benefits, challenges and future trends. Int. J. Product. Econom. 145 (1), 409−430.

Miorandi, D., Sicari, S., De Pellegrini, F., Chlamtac, I., 2012. Internet of things: vision, applications and research challenges. Ad Hoc Networks 10 (7), 1497−1516.

Ning, H., 2013. Unit and Ubiquitous Internet of Things. CRC Press, Boca Raton, FL.

Ning, H., Liu, H., Yang, L.T., 2013. Cyberentity security in the internet of things. Computer 46 (4), 46−53.

Oppliger, R., 2011. Security and privacy in an online world. Computer 44 (9), 21−22.

Peris-Lopez, P., Hernandez-Castro, J.C., Estevez-Tapiador, J.M., Ribagorda, A., 2006. M2ap: a minimalist mutual-authentication protocol for low-cost rfid tags. Ubiquitous Intelligence and Computing. Springer, Heidelberg, pp. 912−923.

Perna, M., 2013. Security 101: securing SCADA environments. Retrieved from <http://blog.fortinet.com/post/security-101-securing-scada-environments>.

Pretz, K., 2013. The next evolution of the internet. Retrieved from <http://theinstitute.ieee.org/technology-focus/technology-topic/the-next-evolution-of-the-internet>.

Raza, S., Shafagh, H., Hewage, K., Hummen, R., Voigt, T., 2013. Lithe: lightweight secure CoAP for the internet of things.

Raza, S., Voigt, T., Jutvik, V., 2012. Lightweight ikev2: a key management solution for both the compressed ipsec and the IEEE 802.15. 4 security. Paper presented at the Proceedings of the IETF Workshop on Smart Object Security.

Roe, D., 2014. Top 5 internet of things security concerns. Retrieved from <http://www.cmswire.com/cms/internet-of-things/top-5-internet-of-things-security-concerns-026043.php>.

Roman, R., Najera, P., Lopez, J., 2011. Securing the internet of things. Computer 44 (9), 51−58.

Roman, R., Zhou, J., Lopez, J., 2013. On the features and challenges of security and privacy in distributed internet of things. Comput. Networks 57 (10), 2266−2279.

Sundmaeker, H., Guillemin, P., Friess, P., Woelfflé, S., 2010. Vision and challenges for realising the internet of things: EUR-OP.

Tan, W., Chen, S., Li, J., Li, L., Wang, T., Hu, X., 2014. A trust evaluation model for e-learning systems. Syst. Res. Behav. Sci. 31 (3), 353−365.

Tao, F., Cheng, Y., Xu, L.D., Zhang, L., Li, B.H., 2014. Cciot-cmfg: Cloud computing and internet of things based cloud manufacturing service system.

Wang, F., Ge, B., Zhang, L., Chen, Y., Xin, Y., Li, X., 2013. A system framework of security management in enterprise systems. Syst. Res. Behav. Sci. 30 (3), 287−299.

Wang, K., Wu, M., 2010. Cooperative communications based on trust model for mobile ad hoc networks. IET Informat. Security 4 (2), 68−79.

Weber, R.H., 2013. Internet of things−governance quo vadis? Comput. Law Security Rev. 29 (4), 341−347.

Welbourne, E., Battle, L., Cole, G., Gould, K., Rector, K., Raymer, S., et al., 2009. Building the internet of things using rfid: the rfid ecosystem experience. IEEE Internet Comput. 13 (3), 48−55.

Wieder, B., Booth, P., Matolcsy, Z.P., Ossimitz, M.-L., 2006. The impact of erp systems on firm and business process performance. J. Enterprise Informat. Manage. 19 (1), 13−29.

Xiao, G., Guo, J., Xu, L., Gong, Z., 2014. User interoperability with heterogeneous iot devices through transformation.

Xu, B., Xu, L.D., Cai, H., Xie, C., Hu, J., Bu, F., 2014a. Ubiquitous data accessing method in iot--based information system for emergency medical services.

Xu, L., He, W., Li, S., 2014b. Internet of things in industries: a survey. IEEE Transact. Indust. Informat. 99, 1.

Xu, L.D., 2011. Information architecture for supply chain quality management. Int. J. Product. Res. 49 (1), 183−198.

Yao, X., Han, X., Du, X., Zhou, X., 2013. A lightweight multicast authentication mechanism for small scale iot applications.

Yuan Jie, F., Yue Hong, Y., Li Da, X., Yan, Z., Fan, W., 2014. Iot-based smart rehabilitation system. IEEE Transact. Indust. Informat. 10 (2), 1568−1577.

CHAPTER 2

Security Architecture in the Internet of Things

Shancang Li

2.1 INTRODUCTION

The Internet of Things (IoT) is an extension of the Internet by integrating mobile networks, Internet, social networks, and intelligent things to provide better services or applications to users. The success of IoT depends on the standardization of security at various levels, which provides secured interoperability, compatibility, reliability, and effectiveness of the operations on a global scale (Li et al., 2016). The IoT is able to connect the digital cyberspace and real physical space, in which the radio-connected intelligent sensors have invaded the physical space and these are now embedded even in everything from our toys to our office equipment, to our healthcare systems. It is clearer than ever before that the IoT is able to introduce all the vulnerabilities of the digital world into our real world.

The success of IoT applications and IoT infrastructure significantly depends on the guarantee of the security and vulnerability in the IoT. Most common types of cyber-attacks can be easily applied to IoT, but as IoT will be deeply interwoven in everything in our lives and business, it is becoming necessary to set up and take cyber defense seriously. The IoT security becomes necessary, which has consequently resulted in a need to comprehensively understand the threats and attacks on IoT infrastructure. In this chapter, we will classify the security requirements and vulnerabilities in IoT, besides analyze and characterize intruders and attacks facing IoT infrastructures and services.

The IoT significantly relies on data captured from a number of diverse sensors spread across a geographic region. For example, in the healthcare section, we are starting to see what the IoT will look like with manufacturers embedding network connectivity and intelligence within devices like patient bedside equipment. We can see the beginnings of interconnections between personal and business IoT capabilities, their smart wearables will soon be able to collect information and transmit that information to healthcare

27

Securing the Internet of Things. DOI: http://dx.doi.org/10.1016/B978-0-12-804458-2.00002-0
© 2017 Elsevier Inc. All rights reserved.

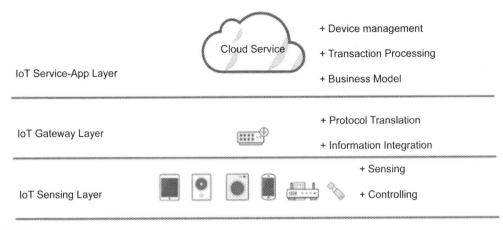

FIGURE 2.1
Structure of a simple IoT system.

providers through the cloud. The transportation sector is another exciting area where the concept of IoT-connected vehicles is sprouting and the infrastructure to support these vehicles is gaining traction. Furthermore, experiments with driverless cars will yield a future where the ability to collect and analyze sensor data from IoT-based roadside equipment will become even important. In many areas, the IoT capabilities have been implemented to meet unique needs and requirements; however, it can also bring security weaknesses and threats. It is important to understand that each unique implementation of IoT should be evaluated for security requirements. In this chapter, we only discuss a generic set of security requirements and vulnerabilities for the IoT; there will always be some level of customization required given the context of each distinct IoT implementation. Fig. 2.1 shows a simple IoT structure that consists of service layer, gateway layer (network layer), and device layer (sensing layer). In the following sections, we will detail the security requirements, authentication/authorization, access control, threats, and attacks in IoT.

2.2   SECURITY REQUIREMENTS IN IoT

The IoT introduces large quantities of new devices that will be deployed or embedded throughout an organization or even within a system. Each connected device could be a potential doorway into the IoT infrastructure or personal data. Data captured from these devices can be analyzed and acted upon. The analysis of this data will allow previously unseen linkages to be made which may cause concern from the privacy of individuals or organization. The data security and privacy concerns are very important but the potential risks associated with the IoT will reach new levels as interoperability, mashups, and autonomous decision-making begin to embed complexity, security loopholes, and potential vulnerability. Privacy risks will arise in the IoT since the complexity may create more vulnerability that is related to the service. In IoT, much information is related with our personal information, such as date of birth, location, budgets, etc. This is one aspect of the big data challenging, and security professions will need to ensure that they think through the potential privacy risks associated with the entire data set. The IoT should be implemented in a lawful, ethical, socially, and politically acceptable way, where legal challenges, systematic approaches, technical challenges, and business challenges should be considered. This paper focuses on the technical implementation design of the security IoT architecture. Security must be addressed throughout the IoT life cycle from the initial design to the services running.

The security has been a big concern in the IoT, but what are the most significant data security and privacy concerns of the IoT are not clearly defined yet. Data security and privacy concerns are not new to the IoT—similar issues have been done from the early days of radio-frequency identification (RFID) adoption. For example, when the electronic passport with RFID tags started equipping passport, the data could be read from as far as 30 ft via equipment available on eBay for $250. The State department had to make changes to the RFID tags and even though the new generation of tags is more secure, the risks associated with the IoT will reach new levels as interoperability, mashups, and autonomous decision-making begin to embed complex, security loopholes and potential "black swan" events.

2.2.1 IoT Data Security Challenges

Similar to the general network systems, Fig. 2.2 shows the security requirements of a simple IoT framework, in which the main security requirements are addressed from six aspects:

- Confidentiality—data secured to authorized;
- Integrity—data is trusted;
- Availability—data are accessible when and where needed;
- Nonrepudiation—service provides a trusted audit trail;
- Authenticity—components can prove their identity;
- Privacy—service does not automatically see customer data.

Privacy risks will arise as objects within the IoT collect and aggregate fragments of data that relate to their service. The collation of multiple points of data can swiftly become personal information as events are reviewed in the context of location, time, recurrence, etc. This is one aspect of the big data

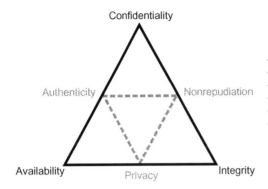

- **Confidentiality**—data is secured to authorized parties
- **Integrity**—data is trusted
- **Availability**—data is accessible when and where needed
- **Nonrepudiation**—service provides a trusted audit trail
- **Authenticity**—components can prove their identity
- **Privacy**—service does not automatically see customer data

FIGURE 2.2

Security requirements in IoT.

challenge, and security professionals will need to ensure that they think through the potential privacy risks associated with the entire data set. The main security challenges in IoT scenario include the data confidentiality, privacy, and trust.

2.2.1.1 Data Confidentiality

- Insufficient authentication/authentication
- Insecure interfaces (web, mobile, cloud, etc.)
- Lack of transport encryption
- Confidentiality preserving
- Access control

2.2.1.2 Privacy

- Privacy, data protection, and information security risk management
- Privacy by design and default
- Data protection legislation
- Traceability/profiling/unlawful processing

2.2.1.3 Trust

- Identity management system
- Insecure software/firmware
- Ensuring continuity and availability of services
- Realization of malicious attacks against IoT devices and system
- Loss of user control/difficult in making decision

To well illustrate the security requirements in IoT, we modeled the IoT as four-layer architecture: *sensing layer, network layer, service layer,* and *application–interface layer.* Each layer is able to provide corresponding security

Table 2.1 Top 10 Vulnerabilities in IoT

Security Concerns	Interface Layer	Service Layer	Network Layer	Sensing Layer
Insecure web interface	✓	✓	✓	
Insufficient authentication/authorization	✓	✓	✓	✓
Insecure network services		✓	✓	
Lack of transport encryption		✓	✓	
Privacy concerns		✓	✓	✓
Insecure cloud interface	✓			
Insecure mobile interface	✓		✓	✓
Insecure security configuration	✓	✓	✓	
Insecure software/firmware	✓		✓	
Poor physical security			✓	✓

controls, such as access control, device authentication, data integrity, and confidentiality in transmission, availability, and the ability to defend IoT devices against virus and attacks. In Table 2.1, the most important security concerns in IoT are summarized.

2.2.2 Security in the Sensing Layer

This layer of the framework is characterized as the intersection of people, places, and things. These things can be simple devices like connected thermometers and light bulbs, or complex devices such as medical instruments and manufacturing equipment. For security in the IoT to be fully realized, it must be designed and built into the devices themselves. This means that IoT devices must be able to prove their identity to maintain authenticity, sign and encrypt their data to maintain integrity, and limit locally stored data to protect privacy. The security model for devices must be strict enough to prevent unauthorized use, but flexible enough to support secure, ad hoc interactions with people and other devices on a temporary basis. For example, you want to prevent someone from changing the toll rate on a connected parking meter, but provide a secure interface to reserve and pay for the parking spot for a limited duration.

Because IoT devices will eventually exist everywhere in the environment, physical security is also important. This creates the need to design tamper resistance into devices so that it is difficult to extract sensitive information like personal data, cryptographic keys, or credentials. Finally, we expect IoT devices to have long lives so it is important to enable software updates to address the inevitable exploits that are discovered after their release.

2.2.3   Security in the Network Layer

This layer of the IoT framework represents the connectivity and messaging between things and cloud services. Communications in the IoT are usually over a combination of private and public networks, so securing the traffic is obviously important. This is probably the most understood area of IoT security, with technology like TLS/SSL encryption ideally suited to solve the problem. The primary difficulty arises when you consider the challenges of cryptography on devices with constrained resources, that is, 8-bit microcontrollers with limited RAM. For example, an Arduino Uno takes up to 3 min to encrypt a test payload when using RSA 1024 bit keys, however an elliptical curve digital signature algorithm with a comparable RSA key length can encrypt the same payload in 0.3 s. This indicates that device manufactures cannot use resource constraints as an excuse to avoid security in their products.

Another security consideration for the network layer is that many IoT devices communicate over protocols other than WiFi. This means the IoT gateway is responsible for maintaining confidentiality, integrity, and availability while translating between different wireless protocols, from Z-Wave or ZigBee to WiFi for example.

2.2.4   Security in the Service Layer

This layer of the framework represents the IoT management system and is responsible for onboarding devices and users, applying policies and rules, and orchestrating automation across devices. Role-based access control to manage user and device identity and the actions they are authorized to take is critical at this layer. To achieve nonrepudiation, it is also important to maintain an audit trail of changes made by each user and device so that it is impossible to refute actions taken in the system. This monitoring data could also be used to identify potentially compromised devices when abnormal behavior is detected.

Big data analysis of the aggregate data generated by IoT is often described as the most valuable aspect of IoT for device and service providers alike. Conversely, maintaining consumer privacy is also top priority for government agencies with the Federal Trade Commission (FTC) and European Union Agency for Network and Information Security (ENISA) releasing their respective guidelines for securing the IoT. This creates a set of privacy-related security requirements such as: providing clear data use notification so that customers have visibility and fine-grained control of the data sent to the cloud service, keeping customer data stored in the cloud service segregated and/or encrypted with customer-provided keys, and when analyzing data in aggregate across customers, the data should be anonymized.

2.2.5   Security in the Interface Layer

There are many challenges to securing the IoT, many unique to each layer of the IoT framework. Robust security begins by building it into the devices themselves. Even small, resource-constrained devices common in the IoT must implement cryptography to maintain confidentiality, integrity, and authenticity when communicating over the network. Finally, a balance between consumer and enterprise privacy and the insight and value derived from the mountains of data generated by the IoT must be found.

We've only scratched the surface of what's required to secure the IoT. Stay tuned as we delve into the specific security models and requirements for each layer of the IoT stack and speculate about how the IoT will evolve in the future.

In Table 2.1, most of the security concerns in different layers of IoT are summarized.

The security requirements depend on each particularly sensing technology, networks, layers, and have been identified in the corresponding sections.

2.2.6   Challenges to Secure IoT

The security solutions have to flip the usual considerations when securing solutions, focusing on delivering availability first, followed by integrity and confidentiality. The challenges include the following:

- Many IoT systems are poorly designed and implemented, using diverse protocols and technologies that create complex configurations.
- Lack of mature IoT technologies and business process.
- Limited guidance for life cycle maintenance and management of IoT devices.
- A long, complex life cycle in which devices are not rebooted often, if ever, makes continuous threat prevention imperative, critical security updates must be delivered while ensuring uptime.
- IoT security solutions often rely on devices that are mass-produced in the same configurations, leaving a broad swath of systems that can be left vulnerable without proper installation and updates.
- Gateways represent a great opportunity to include legacy equipment in IoT, but because these devices were never intended to be connected, they do not have even the most basic security protections. The gateway needs to act as a "helper" to protect the edge.
- IoT is a very big space. When thinking about a solution, we need to consider security at the device level, the connectivity level, and the cloud level in order to understand the potential threats to deployments.

- IoT device could be used in different environments with vastly different risk profiles. For example, a temperature sensor might be used in a home or in a nuclear reactor, each with very different device security, data protection, and encryption needs.
- M2M communication presents a bigger challenge in terms of device identity. Security solutions have to verify the veracity of device data and identity while also ensuring data are protected as it travels to the cloud.

2.3   INSUFFICIENT AUTHENTICATION/AUTHORIZATION

2.3.1   Authentication in IoT

At the heart of this framework is the authentication layer, used to provide and verify the identify information of an IoT entity. When connected IoT/M2M devices (e.g., embedded sensors and actuators or endpoints) need access to the IoT infrastructure, the trust relationship is initiated based on the identity of the device. The way to store and present identity information may be substantially different for the IoT devices. Note that in typical enterprise networks, the endpoints may be identified by a human credential (e.g., username and password, token or biometrics). The IoT/M2M endpoints must be fingerprinted by means that do not require human interaction. Such identifiers include RFID, shared secret, X.509 certificates, the MAC address of the endpoint, or some type of immutable hardware based root of trust.

Establishing identity through X.509 certificates provides a strong authentication system. However, in the IoT domain, many devices may not have enough memory to store a certificate or may not even have the required CPU power to execute the cryptographic operations of validating the X.509 certificates (or any type of public key operation).

Existing identity footprints such as 802.1AR and authentication protocols as defined by IEEE 802.1X can be leveraged for those devices that can manage both the CPU load and memory to store strong credentials. However, the challenges of the new form factors, as well as new modalities, create the opportunity for further research in defining smaller footprint credential types and less compute-intensive cryptographic constructs and authentication protocols.

2.3.2   Authorization

The second layer of this framework is authorization that controls a device's access throughout the network fabric. This layer builds upon the core authentication layer by leveraging the identity information of an entity. With authentication and authorization components, a trust relationship is established between IoT devices to exchange appropriate information. For example, a car may establish a trust alliance with another car from the same vendor. That trust relationship, however, may only allow cars to exchange their safety capabilities. When a trusted alliance is established between the same car and its dealer's network, the car may be allowed to share additional information such as its odometer reading, last maintenance record, etc.

Fortunately, current policy mechanisms to both manage and control access to consumer and enterprise networks map extremely well to the IoT/M2M needs. The big challenge will be to build an architecture that can scale to handle billions of IoT/M2M devices with varying trust relationships in the fabric. Traffic policies and appropriate controls will be applied throughout the network to segment data traffic and establish end-to-end communication.

2.3.3   Insufficient Authentication/Authorization

On the Internet, the users are always authenticated by requiring a password and browsers authenticate web sites through the SSL (secure sockets layer protocol). In the IoT, new devices that connected into an IoT system should be able to authenticate itself prior to receiving or transmitting data. Deeply embedded devices often do not have users sitting behind keyboards, waiting to input the credentials required to access the network. How, then, can we ensure that those devices are identified correctly prior to authorization? Just as user authentication allows a user to access a corporate network based on user name and password, machine authentication allows a device to access a network based on a similar set of credentials stored in a secure storage area.

Assuring the security of each component within an IoT system is important to keep malicious actors from taking advantage of the power of the IoT in an unauthorized manner. In the IoT, some new threats and attack vectors that malicious actors could take advantage of are as follows:

In IoT-based industrial control system, such as SCADA, implantable, manufacturing plants, and other cyber-physical implementation of the IoT:

- Control systems, vehicles, and even the human body (WBAN) can be accessed and manipulated causing injury or worse.
- Healthcare providers can improperly diagnose and treat patients based on modified health information or manipulated sensor data.
- Intruders can gain physical access to homes or commercial businesses through attacks against electronic, remote controlled door lock mechanisms.

2.3.3.1   Individual

- Unauthorized tracking of people's locations can occur through usage pattern tracking based on asset usage time and duration. Unauthorized tracking of people's behaviors and activities can occur through examination of location-based sensing data that exposes patterns and allows analysis of activities, often collected without explicit notice to the individual.
- Unlawful surveillance through persistent remote monitoring capabilities offered by small-scale IoT devices.
- Inappropriate profiles and categorizations of individuals can be created through examination of network and geographic tracking and IoT metadata.

2.3.3.2   Business Area

- Inappropriate profiles and categorizations of individuals can be created through examination of network and geographic tracking and IoT metadata.
- Manipulation of financial transactions through unauthorized POS and POS access.
- Monetary loss arising from the inability to provide service.
- Vandalism, theft, or destruction of IoT assets that are deployed in remote locations and lack physical security controls.

2.3.3.3   Ability to Access the IoT

- Ability to gain unauthorized access to IoT edge devices to manipulate data by taking advantage of the challenges related to updating software and firmware of embedded devices (e.g., embedded in cars, houses, medical devices).
- Ability to gain unauthorized access to the Enterprise network by compromising IoT edge devices and taking advantage of trust relationships.
- Ability to create botnets by compromising large quantities of IoT edge devices.
- Ability to impersonate IoT devices by gaining access to keying material held in devices that rely up on software-based trust stores.
- Unknown fielding of compromised devices based on security issues within the IoT supply chain.

2.3.4   Insufficient Device Authentication in IoT

The IoT devices must authenticate to the local gateway when sending the captured information or perform some actions. The gateway should be able to authenticate to the cloud endpoint when forwarding this data. Applications in IoTs that are able to analyze and render these data must also authenticate to the cloud when requesting the data. The only scalable model for all the above authentications is through security tokens—one actor authenticates to another by including a previously obtained token on its message. The token serves to identify the first actor, enabling the second to make an appropriate authorization decision.

- User authentication, the relevant users should be in control of how the data are collected, shared, and analyzed.
- Authentication tools: OAuth 2.0 and OpenID Connect 1.0 are two standardized frameworks for authentication and authorization that explicitly support the above model. Both enable the user to explicitly participate in the issuance of tokens to applications seeking user data—health or otherwise—and can thereby enable meaningful privacy control. Additionally, Connect provides built-in discovery and registration mechanisms that are extremely relevant in scaling any architecture to the numbers of actors that IoT will create.

Challenges: One challenge is that OAuth and Connect have only been bound to HTTP thus far. Security experts believe that HTTP is insufficient for many of the interactions in the IoT, particularly those between things/devices and other actors. A new class of protocols has emerged that promise to be better suited than HTTP to such interactions, including MQ Telemetry Transport and Constrained Application Protocol. There have been early explorations of binding OAuth and Connect to this new category of IoT-optimized protocols, but work remains.

2.4 INSECURE ACCESS CONTROL

Most existing authorization frameworks for computer networks and online services are role based. First, the identity of the user is established and then his or her access privileges are determined from the user's role within an organization. That applies to most of existing network authorization systems and protocols (RADIUS, LDAP, IPSec, Kerberos, SSH). Online applications and services commonly rely on HTTP cookies stored in a user's browser after their identity has been verified. Although individual authorization systems may differ in how they establish users' identity or how they map the identity to roles and access restrictions, the mechanism always involves identifying the user.

Next, different forms of resource and access control are applied. Mandatory or role-based access controls built into the operating system limit the privileges of device components and applications so they access only the resources they need to do their jobs. If any component is compromised, access control ensures that the intruder has as minimal access to other parts of the system as possible. Device-based access control mechanisms are analogous to network-based access control systems such as MAD (Microsoft Active Directory): even if someone managed to steal corporate credentials to gain access to a network, compromised information would be limited to only those specific areas of the network authorized by particular credentials. The principle of least privilege dictates that only the minimal access required to perform a function should be authorized in order to minimize the effectiveness of any breach of security.

2.4.1 Role-Based Access Control Systems

The commonly used role-based access control systems in computer systems are not suitable for devices in the IoT. The identity of individual device in role-based access control systems may not be known or may not matter. Access control is typically based on other rules/criteria, such as positions, locations, architectures, and others. It is difficult in IoT to implement even the simplest common scenario, such as that a device may control the light in a room only if it is located in the same room, in this case, a more generic attribute-based access control system is needed. The OAuth is an access control system for applications (not users), but requires that applications prove their identity by submitting tokens.

2.4.2 Access Control List-Based Systems

The access control list (ACL) is a table that can tell the IoT system all access rights each user/application has to particular IoT end node. Each node or device has a security attribute that identifies its ACL. Fig. 2.3 shows an ACL-based system, in which the most common privileges include the ability to access or control an IoT device.

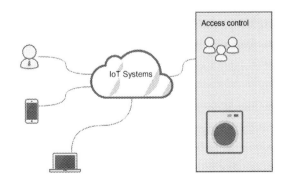

FIGURE 2.3
ACL-based system.

The ACL-based IoT systems refer to rules that are applied to device or device addresses that are available on an IoT system, each with a permitted list of IoT users/applications.

2.4.3 Capability-Based Access

Existing access control methods are not suited for IoT. Consider, for example, FTP where a server listens to a given port at an IP address, both of which are public information. Anyone can connect to the server at this stage. To restrict access, we additionally have a username and a password, which provide the required security. This approach, an embodiment of an ACL, is not scalable as more and more users join and are revoked (Computerworld, 2010; ETSI TR103 167 v0.3.1, 2011). Furthermore, the complexity of managing the ACL also rests on the endpoint—the device—which can be a bottleneck. A more scalable and secure approach is to use "capabilities" (ETSI TR103 167 v0.3.1, 2011; Duqu, 2011). Essentially, a capability is a cryptographic key that gives access to some ability (in our case, to communicate) (Fig. 2.4).

The IoT system relies upon the end nodes that collect information, data, or perform some actions. These IoT end-nodes are able to take the form of standalone devices, for example, intelligent sensor or smart meters, or be embedded in a large system for information capturing, such as connected vehicles, control systems, etc. The data collected, stored, and processed by these IoT end-nodes can also be shared through a backend service, oftentimes, hosted within the cloud. Data analytics systems can make sense of data and in some cases instruct the components to perform some action.

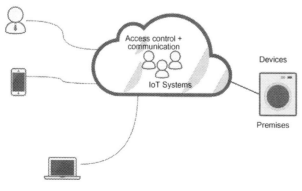

FIGURE 2.4

Capability-based access-based system.

2.4.4 Challenges in Access Control

In access control of IoT, there are a number of challenges, such as weak password, insecure protocols, low-powerful password encryption, etc. We summarized the challenges in access control as follows:

- It is reported that 19% of all tested mobile apps that are used to control IoT devices are not using the SSL connections to the cloud. This can cause attacks from the connection or man-in-the-middle (MIMT) attack.
- Most of the existing devices are unable to provide mutual authentication between the client and the server.
- Strong password support is not supported for many IoT devices.
- Some IoT–cloud interfaces did not support two-factor authentication (2FA).
- Many IoT services did not have lock-out or delaying measures to protect users' accounts against brute-force attacks.
- IoT cloud platforms included common web application vulnerabilities.
- Control IoT devices without performing any deep tests, including unauthorized access to the backend systems.
- Most of the IoT services did not provide signed or encrypted firmware updates, if updates were provided at all.

Actually, the use of weak passwords is a security issue that has repeatedly been seen in IoT devices. In designing an IoT system, we should avoid using weak passwords (Fig. 2.5).

2.5 THREATS TO ACCESS CONTROL, PRIVACY, AND AVAILABILITY

Table 2.2 summarizes the potential security threats and security vulnerabilities at IoT end-node and Table 2.3 analyses the security threats and vulnerabilities in sensing layer.

To secure devices in this layer before users are at risk, following actions should be taken: (1) Implement security standards for IoT and ensure all devices are produced by meeting specific security standards; (2) Build trustworthy data sensing system and review the security of all devices/components; (3) Forensically identify and trace the source of users; (4) Software or firmware at IoT end-node should be securely designed.

The Open Web Application Security Project's list of top 10 IoT vulnerabilities sums up most of the concerns and attack vectors surrounding this category of devices:

- Insecure web interface
- Insufficient authentication/authorization

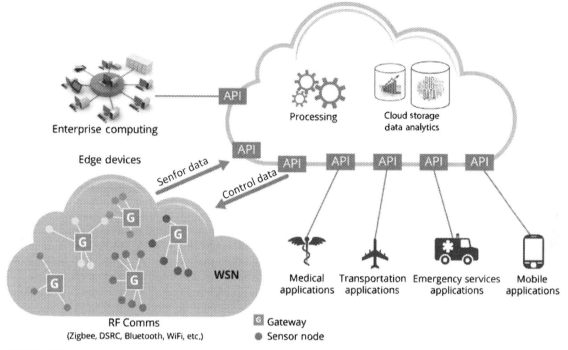

FIGURE 2.5

Example of a WSN-based IoT system.

Table 2.2 Security Threats and Vulnerabilities at IoT End-Node

Security Threats	Description
Unauthorized access	Due to physical capture or logic attacked, the sensitive information at the end-nodes is captured by the attacker
Availability	The end-node stops to work since physically captured or attacked logically
Spoofing attack	With malware node, the attacker successfully masquerades as IoT end-device, end-node, or end-gateway by falsifying data
Selfish threat	Some IoT end-nodes stop working to save resources or bandwidth to cause the failure of network
Malicious code	Virus, Trojan, and junk message that can cause software failure
Denial of Services (DoS)	An attempt to make an IoT end-node resource unavailable to its users
Transmission threats	Threats in transmission, such as interrupting, blocking, data manipulation, forgery, etc.
Routing attack	Attacks on a routing path

- Insecure network services
- Lack of transport encryption
- Privacy concerns
- Insecure cloud interface
- Insecure mobile interface
- Insufficient security configurability
- Insecure software/firmware
- Poor physical security

2.5.1   Threats in Network Layer

The security requirements in network layer involve:

- *Overall security requirements*, including confidentiality, integrity, privacy protection, authentication, group authentication, keys protection, availability, etc.
- *Privacy leakage*. Since some IoT devices are physically located in untrusted places, which cause potential risks for attackers to physically find the privacy information such as user identification, etc.
- *Communication security*. It involves the integrity and confidentiality of signaling in IoT communications.
- *Overconnected*. The overconnected IoT may run risk of losing control of the user. Two security concerns may be caused: (1) DoS attack, the bandwidth required by signaling authentication can cause network congestion and further cause DoS; (2) Keys security, for the overconnected network, the keys operations could cause heavy network resources consumption.
- *MITM attack*, the attacker makes independent connections with the victims and relays messages between them, making them believe that

Table 2.3 Analysis of the Security Threats and Vulnerabilities in Sensing Layer

IoT End-Node Threats and Vulnerabilities	IoT End-Devices	IoT End-Node	IoT End-Gateway
Unauthorized access	√	√	√
Selfish threat		√	√
Spoofing attack		√	√
Malicious code	√	√	√
DoS	√	√	√
Transmission threats			√
Routing attack	√	√	√

they are talking directly to each other over a private connection, when in fact the attacker controls the entire conversation.

- *Fake network message*, attackers could create fake signaling to isolate/misoperate the devices from the IoT.

In the network-layer, the possible security threats are summarized in Table 2.4 and in Table 2.5 the potential security threats and vulnerabilities are analyzed.

The network infrastructure and protocols developed for IoT are different with existing IP network, special efforts are needed on following security concerns: (1) Authentication/Authorization, which involves vulnerabilities such as password, access control, etc. and (2) Secure transport encryption is crucial to encrypt the transmission in this layer.

2.5.2 Threats in Sensing Layer

The security requirements in the service layer include:

- Authorization, service authentication, group authentication, privacy protection, integrity, integrity, security of keys, nonrepudiation, antireplay, availability, etc.

Table 2.4 Security Threats in Network Layer

Security Threats	Description
Data breach	Information release of secure information to an untrusted environment
Transmission threats	The integrity and confidentiality of signaling
DoS	An attempt to make an IoT end-node resource unavailable to its users
Public key and private key	The comprise of keys in networks
Malicious code	Virus, Trojan, and junk message that can cause software failure
DoS	An attempt to make an IoT end-node resource unavailable to its users
Transmission threats	Threats in transmission, such as interrupting, blocking, data manipulation, forgery, etc.
Routing attack	Attacks on a routing path

Table 2.5 The Security Threats and Vulnerabilities in Network Layer

	Privacy Leakage	Confidentiality	Integrity	DoS	PKI	MITM	Request Forgery
Physically protection	√	√					√
Transmission security		√	√	√	√	√	√
Overconnected			√	√	√		
Cross-layer fusion	√	√				√	√

- Privacy leakage. The main concern in this layer involves privacy leakage and malicious location tracking.
- Service abuses, in IoT the service abuse attack involves: (i) illegal abuse of services; (ii) abuse of unsubscribed services.
- Node identify masquerade.
- DoS attack.
- Replay attack, the attacker resends the data.
- Service information sniffer and manipulation.
- Repudiation in service layer, it includes the communication repudiation and services repudiation.

The security solution should be able to protect the operations on this layer from potential threats. Table 2.6 summarizes the security threats on the service layer.

Ensure the data in service layer secure is crucial but difficult. It involves fragmented, full of competing standards and proprietary solutions. The service oriented architecture is very helpful to improve the security of this layer (Atzori et al., 2010; Esad-Djou, 2014), but following challenges still need to be faced when building an IoT services or application: (1) data transmission security between service and/or layers; (2) secure services management, such as service identification, access control, services composite, etc.

Table 2.7 summarizes the security threats and vulnerabilities in IoT application–interface layer.

In Table 2.8, we analyze the security threats and potential vulnerabilities in application–interface layer.

Table 2.6 The Security Threats in Service Layer

Security Threats	Description
Privacy threats	Privacy leakage or malicious location tracking
Services abuse	Unauthorized uses access services or the authorized users access unsubscribed services
Identity masquerade	The IoT end-device, node, or gateway are masqueraded by attacker
Service information manipulation	The information in services is manipulated by the attacker
Repudiation	Denial of the operations have been done
DoS	An attempt to make an IoT end-node resource unavailable to its users
Replay attack	The attack resends the information to spoof the receiver
Routing attack	Attacks on a routing path

Table 2.7 The Security Threats in Application—Interface Layer

Security Threats	Description
Remote configuration	Fail to configure at interfaces
Misconfiguration	Misconfiguration at remote IoT end-node, end-device, or end-gateway
Security management	Log and keys leakage
Management system	Failure of management system

Table 2.8 The Security Threats and Vulnerabilities in Application—Interface Layer

	Unauthorized Access	Failure of Node	Masquerade	Selfish Node	Trojan, Virus, Spam	Privacy Leakage
Physically security protection	√	√	√			
Antivirus, firewalling				√		
Access control	√	√	√			√
Confidential	√	√	√			√
Data integrity		√	√	√	√	
Availability						
Authentication	√	√	√			√
Nonrepudiation	√	√	√			√

The application—interface layer bridges the IoT system with user applications, which should be able to ensure that the interaction of IoT systems with other applications or users are legal and can be trusted.

2.5.3   Threats in Cross-Layer and Maintenance of IoT

Information in the IoT architecture might be shared among all of the four layers to achieve full interoperability between services and devices. It brings a number of security challenges such as trust guarantee, privacy of the users and their date, secure data sharing among layers, etc. In the IoT architecture described in Fig. 2.2, information is exchanged between different layers, which may cause potential threats as shown in Table 2.9.

The security requirements in this layer include (1) security protection, securing to be ensured at design and execution time; (2) privacy protection, personal information access within IoT system, privacy standards, and enhancement technologies; (3) trust has to be a part of IoT architecture and must be built in.

Table 2.9 Security Threats Between Layers in the IoT Architecture

Security Threats	Description
Sensitive information leakage at border	The sensitive information might be not protected at the border of layers.
Identity spoofing	The identities in different layers have different priorities.
Sensitive information spreads between layers	Sensitive information spreads at different layers and cause information leakage

Table 2.10 Security Threats Between Layers in the IoT Architecture

Security Threats	Description
Remote configuration	Fail to configure remote IoT end-node, end-device, or end-gateway
Misconfiguration	Misconfiguration at remote IoT end-node, end-device, or end-gateway
Security management	Log and keys leakage at IoT end-node
Management system	Failure of management system

The maintenance of IoT can cause security problems, such as in configuration of the network, security management, and application managements. Table 2.10 summarized the potential threats that can cause risk in IoT.

2.6 ATTACKS SPECIFIC TO IoT

IoT applications might be subjected to most types of network attacks, including eavesdropping, data modification, identity spoofing, password-based attacks, DOS attack, man-in-the-middle (MITM) attack, compromised-key attack, sniffer attack, and application layer attack. Actually, more specific attacks to IoT have been emerged in recent. Attackers can intercept or change the behavior of smart home devices in many ways. Some methods require physical access to the device, making an attack more difficult to conduct. Other attacks can be carried out over the Internet from a remote location. The following sections list the different attack scenarios based on the access level that the attacker may have.

2.6.1 Physical Access

An attacker can gain the highest level of access to the smart home device if they get physical access to it. Although this might seem like an improbable attack vector, it is still a plausible threat. Your friends could gain physical access to your IoT device to play a prank while visiting you. An ex-boyfriend or girlfriend could attempt to reconfigure some of the devices while they still have access to the home. For some devices, such as security camera, an attacker could simply cut the cables to turn them off.

Another plausible physical access attack scenario takes advantage of the market for second-hand IoT devices. Some users might buy a used device off the Internet in order to save some money, but could end up with a device that has been compromised to spy on people.

Smart home devices could also be compromised through supply chain hacks. In this scenario, attackers compromise a supplier company's network and Trojanize their software updates, allowing the threat to spread to any device that avails of the poisoned update. This is not a new scenario; we have seen attack groups conduct supply-chain attacks to spread their malware to traditional computers many times before, such as during some of the Hidden Lynx attackers' campaigns. Unfortunately, there is currently no easy way to verify that an IoT device has not been tampered with.

Having physical access to the device allows the attacker to alter configuration settings. These could include issuing a new device pairing request, resetting the device to factory settings and configuring a new password, or installing custom SSL certificates and redirecting traffic to a server controlled by the attacker.

Physical access may also allow a skilled attacker to read the device's internal memory and its firmware. They could do this by accessing programmatic interfaces left on the circuit board, such as JTAG and RS232 serial connectors. Some microcontrollers may have disabled these interfaces, but could still allow direct reads from the attached memory chips if the attacker solders on new connection pins.

Reading the internal memory and reversing the firmware allows an attacker to better understand how a device works, allowing them to find vulnerabilities, cryptographic key materials, back doors, or design flaws that could be used to perform further attacks. If the attacker gains a full understanding of the firmware, they could use this knowledge to create their own malicious version of the firmware and upload it to the device. This could give the attacker full control over the device. This act of reflashing the device may be conducted through the JTAG or RS232 connection.

Most new devices offer ways for users to update the firmware throughout the life cycle of the device. These updates could arrive through a USB connection, an SD card, or over the network. The majority of tested devices did not use encrypted nor digitally signed firmware updates, making it easy for an attacker to generate a valid, malicious firmware update that could be installed.

2.6.2   Local Attacks Over WiFi

An attacker with access to the local home network, either wirelessly or through an Ethernet connection, is able to perform various attacks against smart home devices. There are generally two common modes of smart home devices: cloud polling and direct connection. Depending on the function, the device may use either of these methods to receive commands.

References

Atzori, L., Iera, A., Morabito, G., 2010. The Internet of Things: A Survey. Computer Networks 54 (15), 2787−2805.

Computerworld, September 16, 2010. Siemens: Stuxnet worm hit industrial systems.

Duqu: A Stuxnet-like malware found in the wild, technical report, October 14, 2011, Laboratory of Cryptography of Systems Security.

ETSI TR103 167 v0.3.1, 2011. Machine to machine communications (M2M): threat analysis and counter-measures to M2M service layer.

Esad-Djou, M. (2014). IT-security: weblogic server and oracle platform security services (OPSS). Retrieved from < http://thecattlecrew.wordpress.com/2014/02/17/it-security-weblogic-server_1/ > .

Li, S., Tryfonas, T., Li, H., 2016. The internet of things: A security point of view. Internet Research 26 (2), 337−359.

CHAPTER 3

Security and Vulnerability in the Internet of Things

Shancang Li

In this chapter, we will introduce the secrecy and secret-key in the Internet of Things (IoT). We clarify the ways of secret-key generation that the IoT differs from the web application and then highlight the capacity, challenges, and guidance. We also explore the prominent issue of privacy and secrecy. We will discuss fundamental limits on the amount of information that can be reliably communicated in the IoT.

3.1 SECRECY AND SECRET-KEY CAPACITY

The IoT is becoming a key technique in the industrial and the IoT market is in rapid growth, which many IoT devices have been developed to target business and consumer application. In an IoT system, the connectivity between IoT devices, IoT services, and business processes over IoT should be guaranteed with high reliability, security, and performances. Actually, the standardization of IoT is still an open issue. A number of groups are still working to create engineering standards for the IoT and no one company produces all the pieces of IoT such as intelligent sensor, communication protocols, trusted networks, data, IoT services, applications, or even cloud interfaces, etc. However, the IoT devices, communication protocols, and intellectual property should be shared enough so the IoT services can be developed based on an integrated, secure base.

Recently, the lightweight cryptography for IoT has attracted lots of research effort. The traditional cryptography is designed at the application layer without regard to the imperfections of the lower layer. This makes it difficult to directly apply the existing cryptography primitives to the IoT.

Recently, the idea of designing lower layer security schemes, such as physical-layer crypto and lightweight crypto supports the resources (computation, RAM, energy supply, etc.) limited to IoT devices. On the other hand, the

Securing the Internet of Things. DOI: http://dx.doi.org/10.1016/B978-0-12-804458-2.00003-2
© 2017 Elsevier Inc. All rights reserved.

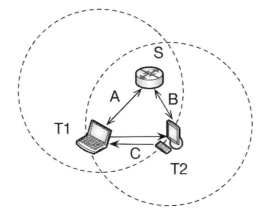

FIGURE 3.1

Example of wireless network with potential eavesdropping.

issues of privacy and security in the network layer of IoT have taken on an increasingly important role as these networks continue to flourish worldwide. The security in IoT is viewed as an independent feature that is closely related with all layers and components of IoT.

In IoT, the application/service desire for secrecy is challenged by the technological need for openness. The idea of physical layer security scheme and lightweight cryptography over resource-limited IoT devices first appeared in the works of Wyner (1975) and Korner (2002). They investigated a channel model by combining the "wiretap channel," in which a transceiver attempts to communicate reliably and securely with a legitimate receiver over a noisy channel, while its messages are being eavesdropped by a passive adversary through another noisy channel. Compare with the Shannon's impracticality of information-theoretic security, the wiretap model has proved the existence of coding schemes achieving information-theoretic secure communications over certain wiretap channels.

Since the nature opened wireless communications are the basic communication way in IoT, which are extremely susceptible to eavesdropping by nature and whose ubiquitous deployment makes security a crucial issue as shown in Fig. 3.1, in which the IoT endpoint T_1 and T_2 can communicate with a sink gateway S over the wireless channels A and B. The endpoint T_2 can listen to the transmission of T_1 through channel C to acquire confidential information. If the endpoint T_1 wants to exchange a secret key or guarantee the confidentiality of its transmitted information, it can exploit the physical properties of the wireless channel to secure the information by coding against endpoint T_2.

The fundamental secrecy limits of various fading wiretap channels have been characterized (Li et al., 2015). The theoretical basis of secrecy capacity (i.e., the

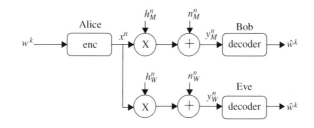

FIGURE 3.2

A simple example of secret capacity over a wireless communication.

maximum transmission rate at which the eavesdropper is unable to properly decode any information) is equal to the difference between the two channel capacities. In this case, the confidential communication is impossible unless the Gaussian main channel has a better signal-noise rate (SNR) then the Gaussian wiretap channel.

Fig. 3.2 depicts a simple example of secret capacity over a wireless communication. A legitimate IoT user Alice hopes to send information w to Bob, who is another legitimate user in the IoT. The information block w^k is encoded into the code word $x^n = [x(1), x(2), \ldots, x(n)]$, which is to be transmitted over a channel with output:

$$y_M(i) = h_M(i) x(i) + n_M(i),$$

in which the $h_M(i)$ is channel side information (the time-varying complex fading coefficient) and $n_M(i)$ is the zero-mean circular complex Gaussian noise. If the third user, Eve, is able to eavesdrop the signal from the open-nature wireless channel:

$$y_W(i) = h_W(i) x(i) + n_W(i)$$

If we use P to denote the average transmit signal power, then the channel is then power limited:

$$\frac{1}{n} \sum_{i=1}^{n} \mathrm{E}\left[|X(i)|^2\right] \leq P$$

The power of noise in the main channel is N_M and the power of noise in the eavesdrop channel is N_W respectively. Then the instantaneous SNR at Bob is:

$$\gamma_M(i) = P|h_M(i)|^2/N_M = P|h_M|^2/N_M = \gamma_M$$

Similarly, the SNR at the Alice is:

$$\gamma_W(i) = P|h_W(i)|^2/N_W = P|h_W|^2/N_W = \gamma_W$$

We can easily get the average SNR based on the above equations. The transmission rate R and error probability P_e^K between Alice and Bob can be defined as:

$R = H(W^k)/n$

and

$$\mathscr{P}_\varepsilon^k = \mathscr{P}(W^k \neq \widehat{W}^k)$$

Then both the maximum transmission rate between Alice and Bob and Eve's uncertainty about w can be calculable. The secrecy capacity of main channel can be defined as the maximum transmission rate R at Δ equals to 1 (Barros and Rodrighues, 2006).

Recently, some research works have been conducted on characterizing the secret capacity over different communication systems, which is crucial for IoT systems where more communication systems exist together to support IoT devices. Based on secrecy capacity, it is possible to develop secure schemes such as key agreement to be done. It can be expected the secure key agreement protocols can be developed over this structure and can bring an IoT system robust authentication scheme.

3.2 AUTHENTICATION/AUTHORIZATION FOR SMART DEVICES

Password is a commonly used authentication method. In IoT, secure authentication must be provided to protect the potentially sensitive sensor data being shared over the IoT systems or even in the cloud. Most existing Internet websites are using password and authenticate site through a secure sockets layer (SSL) protocol to provide authentication. However, in IoT it is difficult to use SSL directly since the huge IoT scale. Fig. 3.3 shows an example of IoT system for healthcare applications.

In the above IoT system, many medical devices are connected to the IoT that must authenticate to the sink node before transmitting the captured data out. The sink node (Medical services gateway) can authenticate to the cloud where the IoT resides when forwarding the data. IoT services or applications over the IoT application layer can perform analysis and must also authenticate to the IoT before using the data. In existing IoT scheme, a security token based authentication method is used to do this. In IoT, two methods commonly used for authentications are: one-way authentication and mutual authentication, as shown in Figs. 3.4 and 3.5, respectively.

Recently, the OAuth-based authentication schemes in IoT have been reported. The OAuth is an open standard for authorization. It is commonly used for

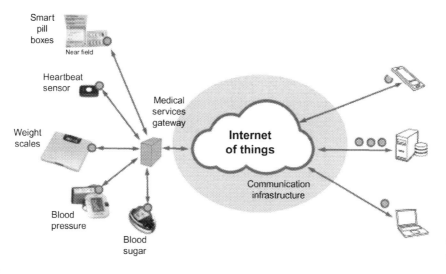

FIGURE 3.3

An example of healthcare IoT system.

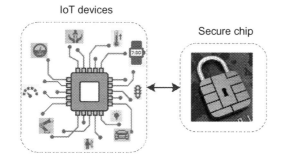

FIGURE 3.4

One-way authentication.

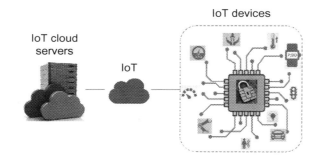

FIGURE 3.5

Mutual authentication.

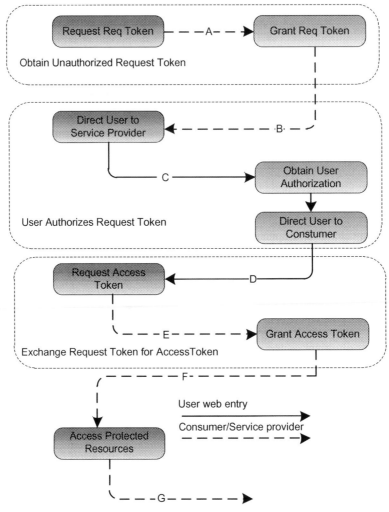

FIGURE 3.6

OAuth flow (left is the user and right is the service provider).

logging in the third-party website without exposing their password. It provides user a secure delegated access to the server on behalf of a resource owner. Fig. 3.6 shows an example of OAuth authentication.

In Fig. 3.6, the solid arrow line denotes user using web browser or manual entry, and the dash arrow line denotes the data flow between user and service provider. In Fig. 3.6, the details are given to address the data flow in Fig. 3.7.

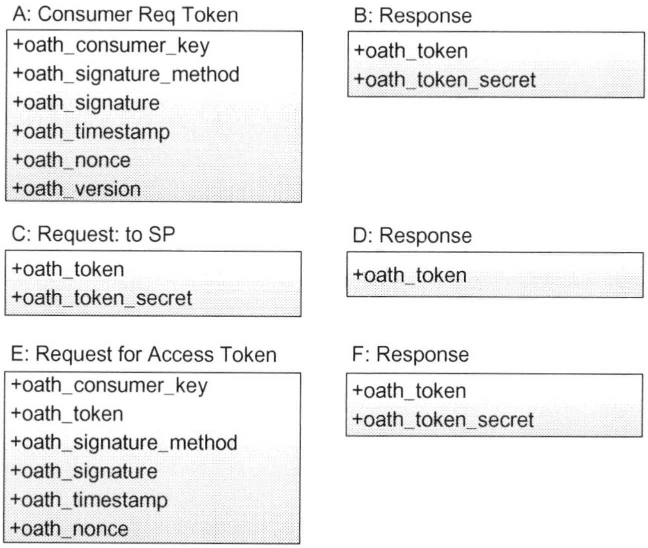

A: Consumer Req Token

+oath_consumer_key
+oath_signature_method
+oath_signature
+oath_timestamp
+oath_nonce
+oath_version

B: Response

+oath_token
+oath_token_secret

C: Request: to SP

+oath_token
+oath_token_secret

D: Response

+oath_token

E: Request for Access Token

+oath_consumer_key
+oath_token
+oath_signature_method
+oath_signature
+oath_timestamp
+oath_nonce

F: Response

+oath_token
+oath_token_secret

FIGURE 3.7
Basic steps of OAuth flow.

The OAuth provides application program interfaces (APIs) for the IoT applications and the OAuth is able to benefit IoT services/applications and user by:

- Allowing untrusted application to perform actions on behalf of an IoT user or end-node at the API provider;
- Authenticating the devices/users permission to perform actions without divulging the user's password;
- Granting specific permissions to untrusted users.

The OAuth 2.0 is believed to be the next generation of authentication for Web applications; it is not compatible with OAuth 1.0 but focuses on users by providing specific authorization flows for applications, mobile phones, or IoT users/devices/services. However, there are still challenges for using OAuth 2.0 in IoT:

- Trusted credentials and standard APIs. In some IoT applications, the digital ID issued by state organizations to identify the user/device.
- Central permission management. Most IoT end-nodes have its own security management interface that makes it very difficult to manage.
- Cloud interface.

OpenID is an open standard for decentralized authentication protocol; it allows users to be authenticated by co-operating site using a third-party services. In IoT, OpenID is a prospective way for devices authentication. Fig. 3.8 shows an example of using OpenID authentication and Fig. 3.9 shows an example of OAuth authentication.

FIGURE 3.8
OpenID authentication.

FIGURE 3.9
Pseudo-authentication using OAuth.

It can be seen that for both OpenID and OAuth, the basic processes are similar:

- Requests for login
- Check if the requester is authenticated
- Redirect URL for the identity provider
- Identity provider authenticates the user
- Provider processes the request and response by sending a back redirect URL to the requester
- Requester response

3.3 TRANSPORT ENCRYPTION

The transport encryption involves the transport layer security (TLS), certificates, and identify verification. Both the TLS and SSL are cryptographic protocols that provide communications security over a network. A properly designed transport protocol can ensure that data, key handshaking, and data integrity verification are encrypted using secure transport protocols such as TLS and SSL. The most common encryption methods we are using in computer networks are mainly based on three algorithms: SSL, TLS, and HTTPS.

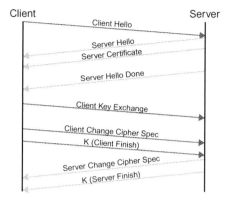

FIGURE 3.10
Establish a TLS connection.

3.3.1 Transport Layer Security

In a TLS communication, to establish a TLS connection between a user and a server needs a typical handshake, as shown in Fig. 3.10; the basic processes are as follows:

1. The user (client) asks request to server.
2. The server sends its certificate to the user.
3. The user ensures that the HTTP server's identity is correct by encrypting a "premaster secret" and if the server can decrypt it correctly, then the user knows the server has the private key matching the public key in the HTTP server's certificate.
4. Both the user and the server send a final finish message to verify that the other side is using the same session key.

3.3.2 Secure Sockets Layer

Fig. 3.11 shows a basic SSL connection. The basic SSL connection involves following four basic steps:

1. User (client) secure connection request
2. Server response to secure request
3. User (client) response
4. Secure channel setup.

The SSL can provide IoT enough transport security.

3.3.3 HTTPS

HTTPS is also called HTTP over TLS/SSL or secure HTTP. It is a protocol for secure HTTP connections and is designed for authentication of the visited

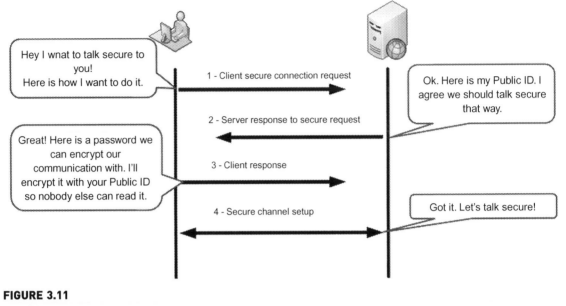

FIGURE 3.11

Basic SSL connection.

website and protection of the privacy and integrity of the exchanged information.

The HTTPS is able to protect against attacks like man-in-the-middle (MITM), eavesdropping, tampering, forging the content, and to provide bidirection encryption between the sender and the receiver. Fig. 3.12 shows an example between a HTTP webserver and a client.

3.3.4 Transport Trust in IoT

In IoT, a number of lightweight protocols have been developed to match the needs of security, transmission, and resource consumption. The Message Queuing Telemetry Transport (MQTT) and Constrained Application Protocol (CoAP) are the two most promising resource limited devices in IoT. Both MQTT and CoAP have following features:

- Are open standard
- Easy to implement
- Provide bandwidth-efficient and uses energy-efficient communication

In Fig. 3.13, the server authentication, client authentication, confidentiality, and IoT protocols have been listed.

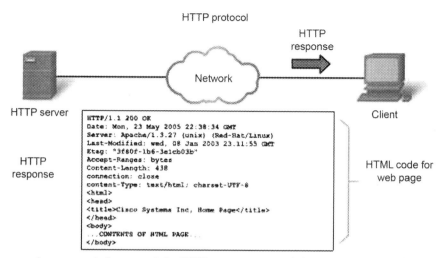

HTTP protocol
HTTP response
Network
HTTP server
Client
HTTP response
HTTP/1.1 200 OK
Date: Mon, 23 May 2005 22:38:34 GMT
Server: Apache/1.3.27 (unix) (Red-Hat/Linux)
Last-Modified: wed, 08 Jan 2003 23.11:55 GMT
Etag: "3f80f-1b6-3e1cb03b"
Accept-Ranges: bytes
Content-Length: 438
connection: close
content-Type: text/html; charset-UTF-8
<html>
<head>
<title>Cisco Systems Inc, Home Page</title>
</head>
<body>
...CONTENTS OF HTML PAGE...
</body>
HTML code for web page
In response to the request, the HTTP server returns code for a web page.

FIGURE 3.12
Example of HTTPS.

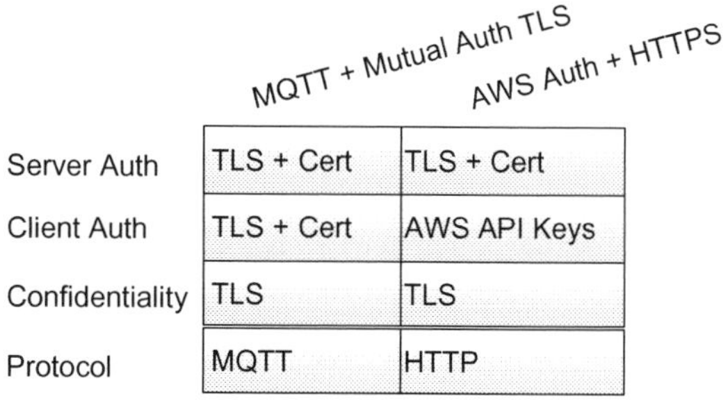

MQTT + Mutual Auth TLS
AWS Auth + HTTPS
Server Auth
TLS + Cert
TLS + Cert
Client Auth
TLS + Cert
AWS API Keys
Confidentiality
TLS
TLS
Protocol
MQTT
HTTP

FIGURE 3.13
Transport security of IoT.

3.4 SECURE CLOUD/WEB INTERFACE

The rapid expanding IoT is expected to interconnect billions of intelligent devices and hence to enhance the business processing. The cloud is playing a key role in the IoT for providing secure connectivity between physical devices and applications. Fig. 3.14 shows a basic structure of IoT-Cloud, in which IoT end-nodes (such as sensors, actuators, smart machines, etc.) securely connect to Cloud through secure cloud/web interface.

IoT Devices and Sensors

IoT-Cloud

Data analysis

FIGURE 3.14

IoT-cloud structure.

In Fig. 3.14, the machine-to-machine (M2M) gateway connects the IoT devices, network systems, and users/applications to the IoT-cloud. Since the IoT infrastructures are becoming complex and both the public cloud and private clouds are built in, which can significantly reduce the threat intelligence and defense capabilities. The basic components within the IoT-cloud include the following:

- The actual IoT M2M gateway from which telemetry and reconnaissance data are required and gathered;
- The Rules engine analyzes the data for the purpose of providing visibility, contextual awareness, and control;
- The secure connection.

Fig. 3.15 shows an example of cloud-based IoT services, in which the connectivity between IoT infrastructures, user/application services, and cloud service and must be designed in a very secure way to protect the private data.

3.5 SECURE SOFTWARE/FIRMWARE

In IoT systems, the hardware secure can benefit the IoT applications:

- Robust IoT end-node and infrastructure can be combined with ease of management for end users.
- New business opportunities in security-sensitive markets such as industrial automation and smart homes.
- Implement layered security protections to defend IoT assets and application level Quality of Service (QoS).

In implementing IoT capabilities, the IoT structure should be tailored to IoT-specific characteristics to allow early adopters of the IoT to mitigate many of

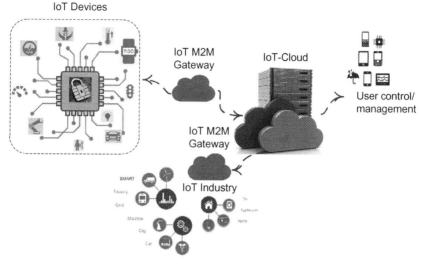

FIGURE 3.15
IoT-cloud-based system.

the risks associated with this new technology. Basically, the security control involves following basic components:

Cryptography Key Management

- Cryptography primitives and controls, include confidentiality/ encryption, integrity, and authentication
- Crypto material and variable, symmetric key, random numbers, entropy source/pool
- Key management, includes key storage/agreement, key material accounting

Protocols

- Application layers, App authorization/authentication, App data confidentiality, app data integrity
- Network layers, network authorization/authentication, network signaling confidentiality, and integrity
- Device authorization/authentication, devices signaling confidentiality, and integrity

At *Device layer*, the following security alliances need to be guaranteed:

- Device logging/audit
- IoT device secure discovery

- IoT device access control
- Physical security

Many attempts have been made to secure devices with software only. However, software has several inherent and significant weaknesses. Software is based on the program code which can be read, analyzed, or even disassembled.

- The software code can be penetrated, analyzed, and disassembled
- Software-based protection systems, attackers can easily identify secret keys that are built into them
- The combination between software security solution and secured hardware makes the security protection solution become more trustworthy.
- Combine with mobile security

Software can be protected by hardware. Fig. 3.16 shows an example of software/firmware update, in which the IoT devices should be designed to be able to be updated with signed new software/firmware. The basic steps include:

1. Decryption of software/firmware
2. Verification of signature
3. Initiation of update process
4. Update the signed software/firmware.

The potential benefits of the software/firmware update include:

- Increased reliability and security of systems and devices
- Rapid roll-out of updated device software and firmware with additional (revenue-generating) features and bug fixes
- Cost efficiencies through the avoidance of expensive software upgrade recalls and support calls
- Secured service delivery to authorized devices for service provider.

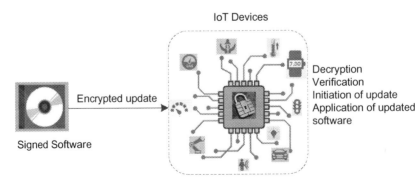

FIGURE 3.16

An example of software/firmware update.

3.6   PHYSICAL LAYER SECURITY

In IoT, the physical layer security has recently become an emerging technique to further improve the security of IoT systems. It is a fundamental and different paradigm where secrecy is achieved by exploiting the physical layer properties of the network system, compared with the existing cryptographic approaches, such as the interference, channel security, thermal noise, etc. Physical layer security features are as follows:

- At the physical layer
- No assumption on adversary's computation power
- No assumption on adversary's available information
- Provable and quantifiable in bits per second per hertz
- Implementable using signal processing, communication, and coding techniques

Fig. 3.17 shows the basic structure of physical security at IoT devices.

In this layer, a number of attacks can be found based on the physical security vulnerabilities and here we summarized several common kinds as follows (Fig. 3.18):

- IoT device capture: the key IoT devices/nodes are controlled easily by the attackers such as gateway, sensors. It can cause all information leaks, including communication keys, and threats of security of the entire IoT systems.
- Fake IoT device: The attackers may add a fake IoT device to the network and input fake code or data to fraud other users or devices.
- Side channel attack: The attackers attack encrypted devices through the side channel leakage information in the process of the device operation, such as the energy and time consumption, radio interferences, etc.

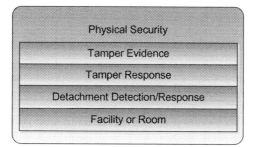

FIGURE 3.17
Components in physical security at IoT devices.

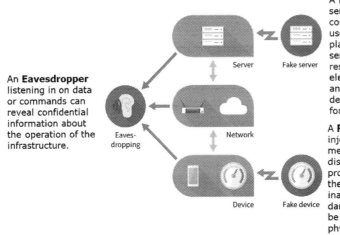

An **Eavesdropper** listening in on data or commands can reveal confidential information about the operation of the infrastructure.

A **Fake server** sending incorrect commands can be used to trigger un-planned events, to send some physical resource (water, oil, electricity, etc.) to an unplanned destination, and so forth.

A **Fake device** injecting fake measurements can disrupt the control processes and cause them to react inappropriately or dangerously, or can be used to mask physical attacks.*
*e.g., BAD USB.

FIGURE 3.18

Fake IoT device attack model.

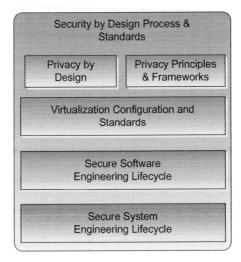

FIGURE 3.19

Security by design processes and standards at IoT devices.

- Timing attack: This kind of attack is based on analyzing the time required for executing encryption/decryption algorithms to obtain the key data.

Practically, the solution for IoT devices security is always a question of trade-off between security, flexibility, performances, energy consumption, and costs. Fig. 3.19 shows the basic components in designing security solutions for IoT devices.

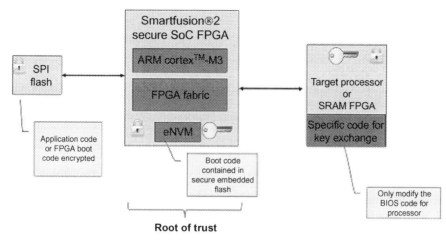

FIGURE 3.20

Hardware security solutions in an IoT system.

Hardware approach security is a secure way to protect IoT devices, which can use hardware chips (such as application-specific integrated circuits (ASICs) or field-programmable gate array (FPGA)) to implement a given cryptography algorithm in hardware. The most commonly used encryption algorithms include RSA, ECC, AES, and 3DES. In RFID security solutions, two security measures are commonly used: Access control and data encryption. In wireless sensor networks, the secret key algorithms and security routing protocols are used to measure the sub-IoT system security.

It is easy to understand that IoT devices are produced by different manufacturers; a sample IoT system main contains components from different manufactures with different security protection solutions. Fig. 3.20 shows an example using hardware security protection approaches.

3.7 SUMMARY

The IoT is growing quickly and a number of smart objectives are brought together, which can bring vulnerabilities in to the IoT systems and may carry serious risks for IoT devices, users, and for IoT-based applications. The hardware-based security solution can secure IoT systems and prevent damages and economic losses offering new opportunities. The IoT hardware security architecture is still in its exploratory stage, so it is facing many severe challenges than expected.

References

Barros, J., Rodrighues, M.R.D., 2006. Secrecy Capacity of Wireless Channels, In: Proceeding of the IEEE International Symposium on Information Theory (ISIT 2006), Seattle, WA, 9–14 July 2006.

Korner, C.I., Korner, J., 2002. Broadcast channels with confidential messages. IEEE Trans. Inf. Theory 24 (3), 339–348.

Wyner, A.D., 1975. The wire-tap channel. Bell Syst. Tech. J. 54, 1355–1387.

Further Reading

Fleisch, E., 2010. What is the internet of things? An economic perspective. Econom. Manage. Financ. Markets 2, 125–157.

Floerkemeier, C., Roduner, C., Lampe, M., 2007. RFID application development with the accada middleware platform. IEEE Syst. J. 1 (2), 82–94.

Furnell, S., 2007. Making security usable: Are things improving? Comput. Security 26 (6), 434–443.

Gama, K., Touseau, L., Donsez, D., 2012. Combining heterogeneous service technologies for building an internet of things middleware. Comput. Commun. 35 (4), 405–417.

Gaur, H., 2013. Internet of things: thinking services.

Gu, L., Wang, J., Sun, B., 2014. Trust management mechanism for internet of things. China Commun. 11 (2), 148–156.

He, W., Xu, L., 2012. Integration of distributed enterprise applications: a survey.

Hendricks, K.B., Singhal, V.R., Stratman, J.K., 2007. The impact of enterprise systems on corporate performance: A study of erp, scm, and crm system implementations. J. Operat. Manage. 25 (1), 65–82.

Hepp, M., Siorpaes, K., Bachlechner, D., 2007. Harvesting wiki consensus: using wikipedia entries as vocabulary for knowledge management. IEEE Internet Comput. 11 (5), 54–65.

Hernandez-Castro, J.C., Tapiador, J.M.E., Peris-Lopez, P., Li, T., Quisquater, J.-J., 2013. Cryptanalysis of the sasi ultra-light weight rfid authentication protocol. arxiv.

Hitt, L.M., Wu, D., Zhou, X., 2002. Investment in enterprise resource planning: business impact and productivity measures. J. Manage. Inform. Syst. 19 (1), 71–98.

Hoyland, C.A., Adams, K.M., Tolk, A., Xu, D.L., 2014. The rq-tech methodology: a new paradigm for conceptualizing strategic enterprise architectures. J. Manage. Analyt. 1 (1), 55–77.

HP Company, 2014. Internet of things research study. <http://digitalstrategies.tuck.dartmouth.edu/cds-uploads/people/pdf/Xu_IoTSecurity.pdf>.

ITU, 2013. The internet of things, international telecommunication union (itu) internet report.

Kang, K., Pang, Z., Da Xu, L., Ma, L., Wang, C., 2014. An interactive trust model for application market of the internet of things. IEEE Trans. Indust. Informat. 10 (2), 1516–1526.

Keoh, S., Kumar, S., Tschofenig, H., 2014. Securing the internet of things: a standardization perspective.

Kim, H., 2012. Security and vulnerability of SCADA systems over ip-based wireless sensor networks. Int. J. Distribut. Sensor Networks 8 (11), 268478.

Klair, D.K., Chin, K.-W., Raad, R., 2010. A survey and tutorial of rfid anti-collision protocols. IEEE Commun. Surv. Tutor. 12 (3), 400–421.

Kranenburg, R.v., Anzelmo, E., Bassi, A., Caprio, D., Dodson, S., Ratto, M., 2011. The internet of things. Paper presented at the 1st Berlin Symposium on Internet and Society (Versión electrónica). Consultado el.

Li, D.X., 2011. Enterprise systems: state-of-the-art and future trends. IEEE Transact. Indust. Informat. 7 (4), 630−640.

Li, F., Xiong, P., 2013. Practical secure communication for integrating wireless sensor networks into the internet of things.

Li, L., Li, S., Zhao, S., 2014. Qos-aware scheduling of services-oriented internet of things.

Li, L., Wang, B., Wang, A., 2014. An emergency resource allocation model for maritime chemical spill accidents. J. Manage. Analyt. 1, 146−155.

Li, S., Xu, L.D., Zhao, S., 2014. The internet of things: a survey. Informat. Syst. Front. 17, 243−259.

Lim, M.K., Bahr, W., Leung, S.C., 2013. Rfid in the warehouse: a literature analysis (1995−2010) of its applications, benefits, challenges and future trends. Int. J. Product. Econom. 145 (1), 409−430.

Miorandi, D., Sicari, S., De Pellegrini, F., Chlamtac, I., 2012. Internet of things: vision, applications and research challenges. Ad Hoc Networks 10 (7), 1497−1516.

Ning, H., 2013. Unit and Ubiquitous Internet of Things. CRC Press, Boca Raton, FL.

Ning, H., Liu, H., Yang, L.T., 2013. Cyberentity security in the internet of things. Computer 46 (4), 46−53.

Oppliger, R., 2011. Security and privacy in an online world. Computer 44 (9), 21−22.

Peris-Lopez, P., Hernandez-Castro, J.C., Estevez-Tapiador, J.M., Ribagorda, A., 2006. M2ap: a minimalist mutual-authentication protocol for low-cost rfid tags. . Ubiquitous Intelligence and Computing. Springer, Heidelberg, pp. 912−923.

Perna, M., 2013. Security 101: securing SCADA environments. Retrieved from <http://blog.fortinet.com/post/security-101-securing-scada-environments>.

Pretz, K., 2013. The next evolution of the internet. Retrieved from <http://theinstitute.ieee.org/technology-focus/technology-topic/the-next-evolution-of-the-internet>.

Raza, S., Voigt, T., Jutvik, V., 2012. Lightweight ikev2: a key management solution for both the compressed ipsec and the ieee 802.15. 4 security. Paper presented at the Proceedings of the IETF Workshop on Smart Object Security.

Raza, S., Shafagh, H., Hewage, K., Hummen, R., Voigt, T., 2013. Lithe: lightweight secure coap for the internet of things.

Roe, D., 2014. Top 5 internet of things security concerns. Retrieved from <http://www.cmswire.com/cms/internet-of-things/top-5-internet-of-things-security-concerns-026043.php>.

Roman, R., Najera, P., Lopez, J., 2011. Securing the internet of things. Computer 44 (9), 51−58.

Roman, R., Zhou, J., Lopez, J., 2013. On the features and challenges of security and privacy in distributed internet of things. Comput. Networks 57 (10), 2266−2279.

Sundmaeker, H., Guillemin, P., Friess, P., Woelfflé, S., 2010. Vision and challenges for realising the internet of things: EUR-OP.

Tan, W., Chen, S., Li, J., Li, L., Wang, T., Hu, X., 2014. A trust evaluation model for e-learning systems. Syst. Res. Behav. Sci. 31 (3), 353−365.

Tao, F., Cheng, Y., Xu, L.D., Zhang, L., Li, B.H., 2014). Cciot-cmfg: cloud computing and internet of things based cloud manufacturing service system.

Wang, F., Ge, B., Zhang, L., Chen, Y., Xin, Y., Li, X., 2013. A system framework of security management in enterprise systems. Syst. Res. Behav. Sci. 30 (3), 287−299.

Wang, K., Wu, M., 2010. Cooperative communications based on trust model for mobile ad hoc networks. IET Informat. Security 4 (2), 68−79.

Weber, R.H., 2013. Internet of things−governance quo vadis? Comput. Law Security Rev. 29 (4), 341−347.

Welbourne, E., Battle, L., Cole, G., Gould, K., Rector, K., Raymer, S., et al., 2009. Building the internet of things using rfid: the rfid ecosystem experience. IEEE Internet Comput. 13 (3), 48−55.

Wieder, B., Booth, P., Matolcsy, Z.P., Ossimitz, M.-L., 2006. The impact of erp systems on firm and business process performance. J. Enterprise Informat. Manage. 19 (1), 13−29.

Xiao, G., Guo, J., Xu, L., Gong, Z., 2014. User interoperability with heterogeneous iot devices through transformation.

Xu, B., Xu, L.D., Cai, H., Xie, C., Hu, J., Bu, F., 2014. Ubiquitous data accessing method in iot-based information system for emergency medical services.

Xu, L., He, W., Li, S., 2014. Internet of things in industries: a survey. IEEE Transact. Indust. Informat. 99, 1.

Xu, L.D., 2011. Information architecture for supply chain quality management. Int. J. Product. Res. 49 (1), 183−198.

Yao, X., Han, X., Du, X., Zhou, X., 2013. A lightweight multicast authentication mechanism for small scale iot applications.

Yuan Jie, F., Yue Hong, Y., Li Da, X., Yan, Z., Fan, W., 2014. Iot-based smart rehabilitation system. IEEE Transact. Indust. Informat. 10 (2), 1568−1577.

CHAPTER 4

IoT Node Authentication

Shancang Li

The IoT aims at enabling a number of next generation technologies, such as intelligent wireless sensor networks (WSNs), smart cities, smart homes, and mobile-health (m-health) systems. These scenarios require secured solutions to prevent leakage of private information and harmful actuating activities by means of peer authentication and secure data transmission between the IoT nodes and servers. However, the existing IP-based IoT structure and primitives are not fully designed with the limitation of resource-constrained IoT devices (such as energy consumption, computation resource, communication ranges, RAM, FLASH, etc.). As a result, more lightweight security solutions are necessary to ensure the security at resource-constrained IoT devices.

In IoT environment, the limitation at IoT end-nodes includes following aspects:

- Processing power, CPU(MCU) processor, RAM
- Storage space
- Network capacity
- Lack of user interface and display
- Energy consumption

In this chapter, we will discuss the following commonly used security protection technologies in constrained IoT environment:

- Security goals in IoT
- Public-key-based authentication
- Identify-based authentication, encryption, and digital signature
- Lightweight cryptography primitives in IoT
- Secure enabling techniques for resource-constrained IoT
- Existing security solutions in IoT

Securing the Internet of Things. DOI: http://dx.doi.org/10.1016/B978-0-12-804458-2.00004-4
© 2017 Elsevier Inc. All rights reserved.

4.1   SECURITY GOALS IN IoT

Similar to existing IP networks, in the different scenarios of IoT, the cryptographic primitives in IoT are utilized to comply with the main security goals for exchanged message and the system itself. The basic security goals in IoT are:

1. Confidentiality: The message is only disclosed to authorized entities, user, nodes, devices, and services; the confidentiality is about the controlling for devices, message access. The private data, keys, and security credentials must be well protected from unauthorized entities.
2. Integrity, the original message is not tampered with: In IoT systems, different applications may have various integrity requirements, such as e-healthcare system may have more restricted data integrity than the general smart cities applications.
3. Authentication and authorization: The connectivity of the devices aggravates the problem of authentication because of the access control and the nature of wireless communication in IoT systems.
4. Availability: The system keeps serving its purpose and stays uninterruptedly available for legitimate entities. The IoT systems are required to be robust to provide services for accessing anytime.
5. Accountability: To improve the robustness of services in IoT environment, accountability of IoT systems is necessary.

Attack techniques in IoT environment are important to understand:

1. Physical attacks, which means attack tampers with physical components. In some case, the IoT devices might be deployed in outdoor environment, which brings risks to IoT systems.
2. Eavesdropping is the process of overhearing an ongoing communication, which is as well preliminary for launching the next two attacks. Since in IoT environment, many IoT end-nodes are interconnected wirelessly and everyone is able to access the medium. Confidentiality is a typical counter-measurement against eavesdroppers. However, if the keying material is not exchanged in a secure manner, the eavesdropper could be able to compromise the confidentiality. Therefore, secure key change algorithms, such as DH (Diffie-Hellman), are used in the practical scenario.
3. Impersonation is when a malicious entity pretends to be another, mostly legitimate, entity, for instance will be replaying a genuine message, in order to bypass the aforementioned security goals. A special form of this attack is the man-in-the-middle (MITM) attack.
4. MITM attack takes place when a malicious entity is on the network path of two genuine entities. Hence, it is capable of delaying, modifying, or dropping messages. MITM attack is interesting within the context of public-key cryptography (PKC). Then the malicious entity

does not attempt to break the keys of involved parties, but rather to become the falsely trusted MITM. The malicious user achieves this by replacing the exchanged keys with its own. This way each of the parties establishes a secure channel with the malicious user, who gains access to messages in plain text.

5. DoS (Denial of Service) attack targets the availability of a system that offers services. This is achieved by exhaustingly consuming resources at the victim so that the offered services become unavailable to legitimate entities. A common way to launch this attack is to trigger expensive operations at the victim that consume resources, such as computational power, memory, bandwidth, or energy. This attack is critical for constrained devices, where existing resources are already scarce.

6. Access attacks that involve attacks unauthorized entities gain access to IoT systems or devices.

7. Other attacks, such as firmware attack as "bad USB," attacks on privacy, RAM attacks, channel side attack, ransomware, etc.

4.2 PUBLIC-KEY-BASED AUTHENTICATION

In IoT, authentication is the process of identifying users, devices, applications, and restricting access to authorized users and nonmanipulated devices or services. In this process, the username and password-based cryptographic schemes are used to provide a robust secure operation over the IoT. The authentication mechanisms can provide the IoT following benefits:

- Robust devices and secure communication for users
- Development of new services over IoT
- Avoidance of embarrassing data breaches
- Strong anticounterfeiting and antitampering capability
- Reduce risk of third-party services

The public-key-based authentication is widely used in current Internet; however, it is impracticable for constrained environment such as IoT due to expensive cryptographic operations. In this section, we will investigate public-key-based authentication and analysis how to tailor it for light cryptographic in constrained IoT environment. The authentication of IoT end-nodes is an important issue to provide basic secure protection of the network and devices. The node authentication in IoT involves the following:

- Smart objects, small device with specific purpose, low cost, limited abilities;
- IoT, interconnect things and their users to enable new applications;
- IoT nodes are expected to be integrated in all aspects of existing works, entrusted with vast amounts of data, need to communicate unseen and autonomously.

Table 4.1 Resources Classification for IoT Nodes

Name	Data Size (e.g., RAM)	Code Size (e.g., Flash)
Class 0, C0	≪10 KiB	≪100 KiB
Class 1, C1	∼10 KiB	∼100 KiB
Class 2, C2	∼50 KiB	∼250 KiB

Existing RFC7228: Terminology for IoT node networks (constrained environment)

- Device classification
- Energy profile
- Sleep strategies

Table 4.1 shows the resources classification for IoT end-nodes.

Cryptography is widely used in networks to protect private communications and a number of ciphers have been developed, such as Data Encryption Standard, the Ron Rivest, Adi Shamir and Leonard Adleman (RSA) was the first practical public-key cryptosystem.

In IoT environment, the communications between nodes and the infrastructure node require light key distribution method using the public key to reduce the burden; however, it is difficult to apply the method to a light device where the encryption module, such as advanced encryption standard (AES), RSA, elliptical curve cryptography (ECC), cannot be mounted. The **internet engineering task force** (IETF) is considering application of transport layer security (TLS), datagram transport layer security (DTLS), IPSec, etc., which have been adopted in the IP-based networks. The basic concept is to apply DTLS to constrained application protocol (CoAP), which is the key protocol in IoT. In this section, we will review the basic concepts of public-key schemes, symmetric cryptography, and its application in encryption. Then, we cover the PKC and public-key infrastructure (PKI), specifically with regard to X.509 certificates and RAW Public Keys (RPKs).

The basic goals of an authenticated authorization protocol in IoT include:

- Secure exchange of authorization information
- Establish DTLS channel between constrained nodes
- Use only symmetric key cryptography on constrained nodes
- Support of class-1 devices
- RESTful architectural style
- Relieve constrained nodes from managing authentication and authorization

The authenticated authorization

- Determine if the owner of an item of interest allows an entity to access this item as requested.
- Authentication: Verify that an entity has certain attributes (cf. RFC4949).
- Authorization: Grant permission to an entity to access an item of interest.
- Authenticated Authorization: Use the verified attributes to determine if an entity is authorized.

4.2.1 Symmetric Cryptography

A symmetric-key system is used to provide confidentiality of message in transmission, storing, and processing. The symmetric-key algorithm performs the operations of encryption/decryption based on a single key that is shared by two or more parties. A difficulty in symmetric cryptography is securely delivering the key from the encoder to the decoder(s) can introduce a security risk. Anyone who gains access to the symmetric key is able to access/modify/send the message without the recipient's knowledge that the message has been modified. To fix these issues, public-key cryptography or asymmetric key have been developed. The symmetric cryptography algorithms are usually grouped into stream ciphers and block ciphers. The AES is a commonly used block cipher encryption algorithm in network security solutions.

In symmetric-key encryption, the secret key K, the plain text message P, and the cipher text C have the same length. For example, in AES 128, the length of K, P, C are all 128 bits (16 bytes), both the encryption and decryption operations consist of XORing, permutations, bit-shifting, and linear mixing functions that are performed in a known order. In general, the original plain text is divided into multiple blocks with fixed length:

$C_i = \text{Encrypt}\,(K,\ P_i), \quad \forall i = 1, \ldots, n$

The weakness of this is that the same plain text blocks result in same cipher blocks. This is especially critical for packets with a known format and a repeating pattern in the content. To introduce randomness into cipher blocks and make decryption attacks difficult, Cipher Block Chaining (CBC) can be used where before encryption each plain text block is Exclusive operation (XORed) with the previous cipher block.

In Fig. 4.1, the first cipher block C_0, which is XORed to the first plain text block as input, is referred to as the initialization vector (IV). Except the IV, all the following cipher blocks are dependent on all the previous cipher blocks due to the XORing. This feature is used in CBC-message authentication code (MAC) to provide authentication and integrity protection. In Fig. 4.1, the last cipher block C_n serves as the MAC.

$C_i = \text{Encrypt}\,(K,\ P_i \oplus C_{i-1}), \quad \forall i = 1, \ldots, n,\ C_i = \text{IV}$

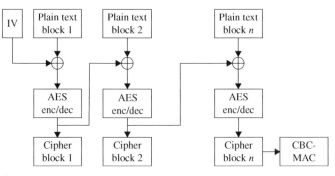

FIGURE 4.1
AES block encryption.

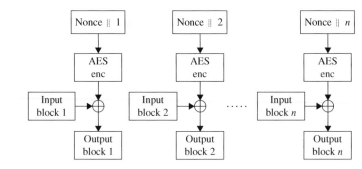

FIGURE 4.2
AES-CTR block encryption.

A MAC provides information that allows to authenticate a message and to verify the integrity of it. Practically, a more typical way than CBC-MAC is used to create the MAC of a message M is by using a hash function with a shared secret key K:

$$MAC(M) = HASH(K|M) = D$$

A secure cryptographic hash function generates from a variable input, a fixed length of output.

The AES-CTR is another block cipher encryption algorithm that, in contrast to CBC, uses a Nonce and a counter to add randomness to each cipher block, as shown in Fig. 4.2.

The input can be a plain text or cipher block and the output is the corresponding cipher or plain text block, respectively.

$$K_i = \text{Encrypt } (K, \text{Nonce}||i), \quad \forall i = 1, \ldots, n$$
$$C_i = P_i \oplus K_i$$

The decryption in counter (CTR) mode is performed in the same fashion as encryption which utilizes the following feature of XOR:

$$C_i \oplus K_i = P_i \oplus K_i \oplus K_i = P_i$$

As a result, CTR does not use AES decryption.

4.2.1.1 AES-CCM

AES-CCM is a mode of operation for block ciphers, which is developed to provide at the same time confidentiality, authentication, and integrity protection. This is achieved by encryption in CTR mode and creating the CBC-MAC of the input. The CBC-MAC is 128 bits but can be truncated to any length. It is then appended to the end of the cipher text. Since CBC-MAC and CTR are performed into separate steps, there is the possibility of selectively not encrypting the entire input, but integrity protecting it entirely. This feature puts **counter with CBC-MAC (CCM)** in the class of algorithm that provides authenticated encryption with associated data.

Since the AES-CCM only relies on AES encryption, most of IoT chips have a hardware built-in AES engine. This makes AES-CCM the favorable choice of encryption for constrained devices or sensors. In IoT, the standardization community requires AES-CCM as the mandatory cipher suite for DTLS in secure CoAP.

4.2.2 Public-Key Cryptography

The symmetric key algorithms are quite efficient, but the key distribution is difficult to IoT end devices. The key distribution requires a secure connection between the key distribution sever and the IoT nodes. PKC and asymmetric cryptography are two effective ways of providing confidentiality and authentication. In contrast to the symmetric cryptography, the PKC is based on mathematically hard problem to solve, whereas hard in this context refers to the complexity of calculation. The public-key encryption is based on "trapdoor" functions, which are easy to compute, but hard to reverse without additional information. The RSA is a widely used public-key algorithm, in which the hard problem is finding the prime factors of a composite number. In PKC cryptosystem, generally in a key pair, the public key and the private key, the public key is made accessible to the public and the private key is kept at a safe place. The public key is generally used in two ways.

1. Public-key encryption, in which one is capable to encrypt a message with the public key of an entity, where only the entity with the corresponding private key is capable of decrypting the cipher text.
2. Digital signatures, in which a cipher text generated with the private key can be decrypted by anyone who has the public key. This verification proves that the sender had access to the private key and therefore is likely to be the person associated with the public key.

Table 4.2 Key Size for Symmetric Key, RSA, and ECC

Symmetric Key	RSA Key	Elliptic Curve Key
80	1024	160
112	2048	224
128	**3072**	**256**
192	7680	384
256	15,360	521

In PKC system, public/private key pairs can be easily generated for encryption and decryption. The security strength in a PKC system lies in how difficult to determine a properly generated private key from its public key. In this case, the length of private key is important for avoiding brute-force attacks.

The RSA is one of the first practical public-key cryptosystems, which is based on the practical difficulty of factoring the product of two large prime numbers. If the public key is large enough, only the one knowing the prime numbers can feasibly decode the message. The RSA is a relative slow algorithm for encryption however it is commonly used to pass encrypted shared keys for symmetric key cryptography. Since RSA encryption is an expensive operation, in IoT it is rather used in combination with symmetric cryptography. The shared symmetric key is encrypted with RSA; the security of encryption in general is dependent on the length of the key. For RSA, a key length of 1024 bits (128 bytes) is required, to have an equivalent security level of symmetric key cryptography with a key length of 128 bit (16 bytes). The large key size of RSA will cause expensive computation costs.

The ECC is an alternative to common PKC because of the resistance against powerful index-calculus attacks. The ECC allows efficient implementation due to a significant smaller bit size of the operands over resource-constrained environment. ECC is another public-key cryptography approach that works based on elliptic curves over finite fields. ECC's smaller key size is 256 as shown in Table 4.2. It is more efficient than RSA and it is more suitable for resource-limited devices in IoT. The basic idea of ECC is the general assumption that the elliptic curve discrete logarithm problem is infeasible or at least not solvable in a reasonable time.

4.2.3 Public Key Infrastructure

A PKI is a set of roles, policies, and procedures needed to create manage, distribute, use, store, and revoke digital certificates and manage public-key encryption (Wiki). In IoT environment, the general public-key problem is the requirement of an authenticated exchange of public keys. The PKI consists of components to securely distribute public keys and is today widely used in the traditional Internet. The most important PKI is a trusted third party who signs the identifier of an entity with its private key.

Interconnected devices in IoT environment must provide trustworthy information to users and services; however, establishing trust across large-scale network is a significant challenge. The devices in IoT are easily attacked and the communications between nodes in IoT are usually difficult to secure. The PKI system works well in existing systems such as banking systems, cellular stations, mobile networks, and are proven to be able to provide trusted environment. So the PKI is a promising solution in IoT.

- PKI comes to assurance and validation.
- Scale. The PKI deployments certainly exist that have the ability to manage millions of certificates, most operate at significantly smaller level.
- Technology issue. Extremely low-power and low-budget device will populate the IoT. Traditional cryptography is not designed for these environments and is mathematically intensive, which requires CPU power. Another problem is credential generation. Making good keys is not easy, and making them in high volumes can quickly become a bottleneck. Again, cryptoalgorithms designed for low-power devices and rapid key generation already exist and have been widely proven.

Before we detail how the PKI works, we first introduce the basic concepts in PKI. The trusted third party is referred to as certification authority (CA) who issues a certificate which mainly constrains the public key and the identifier of an entity. The main elements include:

- Subject: the identifier of the entity whose public key is being certified
- Signature: the algorithm used to create the signature
- Subject PKI: subjects public key and identifier of the algorithm used to generate
- Validity: the time period the certificate can be used
- Issuer: CA's identifier
- Signature value: The issuer's signature on the hash of the previous elements.

Access to the public key of the CA is required to verify the certificate. This brings us in the original problem. Root CAs are at the highest level of trusted hierarchy and have self-signed certificates. Furthermore, root CAs are predeployed into systems for instance via browser vendors.

4.3   IDENTIFY-BASED AUTHENTICATION, ENCRYPTION, AND DIGITAL SIGNATURE

4.3.1   Identify-Based Authentication

Technically, IoT consists of uncountable devices, sensors, or actuators or simply objectives connected to services in the Internet. These objectives are from different vendors, communities, or standard groups. Most of these devices speak different protocols, which make the IoT hard to be implemented. In this case, the devices identify management as one of the most important common technologies, which should be able to coordinate different protocols, standards, scenarios. From a security point of view, security protection should be provided for "Identities of things" in heterogeneous communication and machine-to-machine security. The security challenges are related to identification, authentication, privacy, trustworthiness, and confidentiality. The identification is one of the most important challenges in security of IoT. IoT consists of variety of smart devices like intelligent sensors, smart objectives, computer, back-bone servers, cloud clusters, etc. All of them should be uniquely identified for addressing capabilities and for providing a means to communicate with each other. From the viewpoint of security, the security protection mechanism should be able to identify the message generators, transmitters, and receivers. Existing identification schemes, for example, RFID objective identifier, EPC global, NFC, IPv4, IPv6, etc., have been developed for existing networks, however, how to securely manage devices in IoT environment is still a challenge.

The commonly used protocols for identity authentication include:

- One-way authentication, which authenticates two nodes. For example, node 1 and node 2 have a common secret key X_{uh}. Node selects $r \in GF(P)$ which will be used to create session key. T_u is time stamp of nodes. The secret key created by node 1 is $L = h(X_{uh} \oplus T_u)$, then node 1 encrypts r with L as $R = E_L$ and encrypts T_u with X_{uh} as $T_{us} = EX_{uh}(T_u)$. $\text{MAC}_1 = \text{MAC}(X_{uh}, R||\text{ICAP}_1)$, where ICAP_1 is a data structure represented by an identity based on node 1. Now, node 1 sends the following parameters to node 2 $(R, T_{us}, \text{MAC}_1)$. Node 2 generates its time stamp as T_{current} and decrypt T_{us} to get T_u and compare it with T_{current}. If $T_{\text{current}} > T_u$, it is valid. Now in node 2 calculate L and decrypt R to get r. It also calculates MAC'_1 and it will verify this with MAC_1 received from node 1. Fig. 4.3 shows the protocol.
- Mutual-authentication, which is part of authentication authenticates node 2 to node 1. Node 2 builds a MAC as $\text{MAC}_2 = \text{MAC}(r||\text{ICAP}_2)$ and also encrypts r with X_{uh} as $R' = EX_{uh}(r)$. Then it sends (R', MAC_2) to

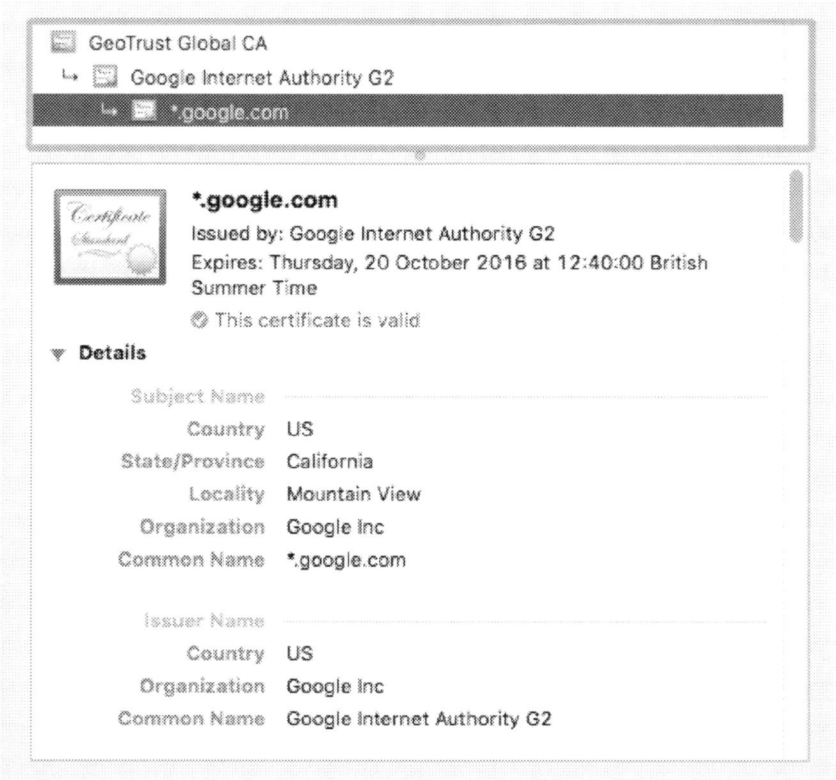

FIGURE 4.3
Example of Google CA.

node 1. Node 1 verifies MAC_2 and decrypts R' and compares received r with this r'. Fig. 4.4 shows the protocol.

Two of the best-known uses of PKC are:

- Public-key *encryption*, a message is encrypted with a recipient's public key. The message can only be decrypted by the matching private key, who is assumed to be the owner of the key and the person associated with the public key. This is used in an attempt to ensure confidentiality.
- Digital signatures. A message is signed with the sender's private key and can be verified by anyone who has access to the sender's public key. This verification provides that the sender had access to the private key, and therefore is likely to be the person associated with the public key. This ensures that the message has not been tampered with.

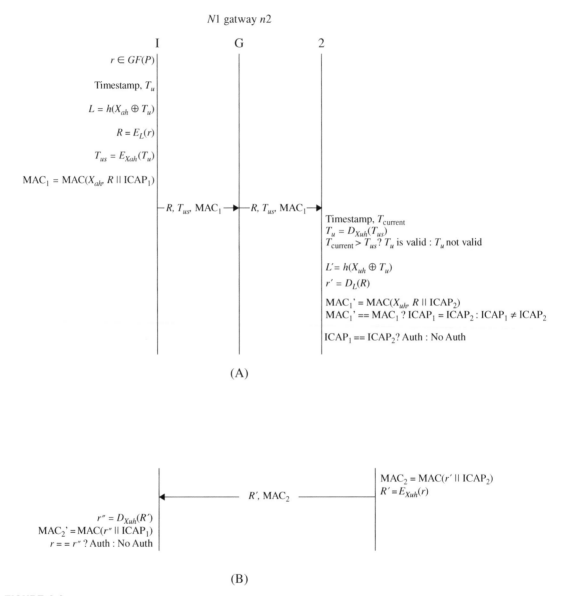

FIGURE 4.4

(A) One-way authentication and (B) mutual authentication.

4.3.2 Digital Signature

A problem with the use of public-key cryptography is confidence/proof that a particular public key is authentic. It is correct and belongs to the person or entity claimed, and has not been tampered with or replaced by a malicious third party.

The usual approach to the problem is to sue PKI, in which one or more third parties—known as CAs—certify ownership of key pairs. To date, no fully satisfactory solution to the "public-key authentication problem" has been found.

The symmetric key algorithms are quite efficient, but the key distribution is difficult at IoT end devices. The key distribution requires a secure connection between the key distribution sever and the IoT nodes. PKC and asymmetric cryptography are two effective ways of providing confidentiality and authentication. In contrast to the symmetric cryptography, the PKC is based on mathematically hard problem to solve, whereas hard in this context refers to the complexity of calculation. The public-key encryption is based on "trapdoor" functions, which are easy to compute, but hard to reverse without additional information. The RSA is a widely used public-key algorithm, in which the hard problem is finding the prime factors of a composite number. In PKC cryptosystem, generally is a key pair, the public key and the private key, the public key is made accessible to the public and the private key is kept at a safe place. The public keys are generally used in two ways.

1. Public-key encryption, in which one is capable of encrypting a message with the public key of an entity, where only the entity with the corresponding private key is capable of decrypting the cipher text.
2. Digital signatures in which a cipher text generated with the private key can be decrypted by anyone who has the public key. This verification proves that the sender had access to the private key and therefore is likely to be the person associated with the public key.

In PKC system, public/private key pairs can be easily generated for encryption and decryption. The security strength in a PKC system lies in how difficult to determine a properly generated private key from its public key. In this case, the length of private key is important for avoiding brute-force attacks.

The RSA is one of the first practical public-key cryptosystems, which is based on the practical difficulty of factoring the product of two large prime numbers. If the public key is large enough, only the one knowing the prime numbers can feasibly decode the message. The RSA is a relative slow algorithm for encryption; however, it is commonly used to pass encrypted shared keys for symmetric key cryptography. Since RSA encryption is an expensive operation, in IoT it is rather used in combination with symmetric cryptography. The shared symmetric key is encrypted with RSA, the security of encryption in general is dependent on the length of the key. For RSA, a key length of 1024 bits (128 bytes) is required, to have an equivalent security level of symmetric key cryptography with a key length of 128 bit (16 bytes). The large key size of RSA will cause expensive computation costs.

The ECC is an alternative to common PKC because of the resistance against powerful index-calculus attacks. The ECC allows efficient implementation due to a significant smaller bit size of the operands over resource-constrained environment. ECC is another public-key cryptography approach that works based on elliptic curves over finite fields. ECC's smaller key size is 256 as shown in Table 4.2. It is more efficient than RSA and it is more suitable for resource-limited devices in IoT. The basic idea of ECC is the general assumption that the elliptic curve discrete logarithm problem is infeasible or at least not solvable in a reasonable time.

The IETF recommends the AES-CCM in combination with ECC for constrained devices. In this section, we will explain how ECC is used to perform a secure key exchange and create digital signatures.

- ECC concept
- Secure key exchange
- Digital signature

The equation of an elliptic curve has the following form:

$$y^2 = x^3 + ax + b$$

The set of EC points are on this curve. A feature of EC is that the result of addition of two points on the curve lies again on the curve. The same holds as well for multiplication. Assume P is a known point on a given EC, and d is a secret random number which serves as the private key, the public key Q, and the private key d have the following relation:

$$Q = d \times P$$

Then, the public key Q is again a point on the same curve. Although Q and P are publicly known and Q is the result of adding P and d times to itself, it is mathematically a hard problem to compute d.

Public keys are created by multiplying the generator. Using the routines for arithmetic, other routines can be built that will compute scalar multiples of the generating point, kP, or of other points $Q = dG$. Public keys are created by multiplying the generator, that is Q is the public key for d if $Q = dP$ on the elliptic curve. Key generation is the production of (d, D) is therefore very basic and efficient in ECC. In RSA key generation involves coming up with large prime numbers and takes much longer.

Assume user Q wants to sign a message m, he/she first computes $K = kP$ for k random, since this can be complete before the message is in hand, so it is often completed over powerful service and passed to the constrained nodes in IoT. If the message m can be signed by computing with much less intensive modular computations over nodes:

$$r = x_{coord}(K = kP) \bmod n$$
$$s = K^{(-1)}(m + dr)$$

in which n is the pointer order and the signature on message m is (r, s). If one knows the public key D, then he can verify this signature on m as:

$$K' = (s^{n-1}m)P + (s^{(-1)}r)Q$$

$$r' = x_{coord}(K')$$

if the r and r' are the same, it means it is acceptable. In practical, the applications that require cryptography system can quickly generate signatures and a number of speeding up verification based on ECC have been developed.

The ECC has small key sizes and is able to generate efficient signature. The strength and efficiency of ECC makes it an ideal for many IoT applications over resource-limited devices. The ECC is suitable for securing IoT environment where more resource-constrained devices are interconnected, such as intelligent sensors, wireless sensor nodes, and e-healthcare devices.

4.3.3 Raw Public Key

In resource-constrained IoT devices, such as intelligent sensors or RFID tag, the certificate chains or even single certificate may be too big to process. Recently, the RPKs are recommended by IEFT instead of the certificates for TLS and DTLS. The RPK requires the out-of-band validation of the public key:

1. Obtaining the public key via DNS-based authentication of named entities or authentication via DNS security extensions
2. Predeployment of RPKs is beneficial in IoT-constrained devices which are configured before deployment with the public key of the back-end service.

The RPK contains the subject Public-Key Information of a certificate which carries the public key values and the algorithm identifier of the cryptographic algorithm used to generate it. RPKs allow for omitting large certificates from the handshake; however, it requires an out-of-band technique for the verification of the public key.

It should be noted that if an IoT gateway node supports the RPK certificates, it must support specific cipher suites such as TLS_ECDHE_ECDSA_WITH_AES_128_CCM_8 (CoAP) and TLS_ECDHE_ECDSA_WITH_AES_128_CBC_SHA256. The end IoT nodes must support at least one of the above cipher suites. The client node uses the value of the "Public Key or Identify" resource for its RPK certificate to determine the expected value of the server's RPK and the value "Secret Key" resource for its private key. The client must check whether the RPK presented by the server exactly matches with the stored public key. The RPK mode is appropriate for IoT nodes deployments where there is an existing trust relationship between the client and server. The server must store its own private and public keys, and must have a stored copy of the expected client public key. The server must check that the RPK present by the IoT client exactly matches with the stored public key. In some application scenarios, such as smartcard, the RPK certificates provisioning needs no preexisting trust relationship between server and client. The preestablished trust relationship is simply between the server and the smartcards.

4.3.4   X.509 Certificates

X.509 is an important standard in cryptography, which is designed for a PKI to manage digital certificates and public-key encryption. The X.509 is a key part of the TLS and it is widely used in web, mobile, and email security. In X.509, an organization that needs a signed certificate requests one via a certificate signing request (CSR). To do this (1) they first generate a key pair, keeping the private key secret and using it to sign the CSR, which contains the public key that is used to verify the signature of the CSR and the distinguished name (DN) and (2) the certification authority issues a certificate binding a public key to particular DN.

The Firefox, Chrome, Safari, etc. come with a predetermined set of root certificates preinstalled, so SSL certificates from large vendors will work instantly. In effect the browsers' developer determine which CAs are trusted third parties for the browser's users (Fig. 4.5).

How SSL works

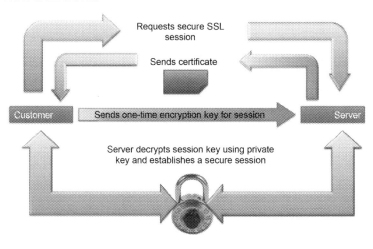

FIGURE 4.5
AES-CTR block encryption.

X.509 certificates are the dominating type of certificates and are consequently used in the certificate-based model of DTLS. In this section, we briefly address the concepts of X.509.

The X.509 certificates are encoded into Base64 which is a binary-to-text encoding scheme. The basic structure is

- *Identifier*
- *Length*
- *Content*

4.4 IP CONNECTIVITY

IoT is a hybrid network that contains different networks: WSNs, Mobile networks, IP, and wireless mesh networks. Most existing IoT solutions are undergoing the IP-enabled and thus connected to the Internet. As a result, existing and matured IP-based security protocol is within constrained environment. Since the existing IP-based security protocol is not designed for resource-constrained devices, such as intelligent sensors, it cannot be used just directly in IoT. It is needed to redesign the existing IP-based protocols or improve it for IoT devices. The TLS is the underlying security protocol for applications protocols, such as HTTP, HTTPS, and it runs over TCP. In IoT, the UDP has become the de facto favorable protocol since it is simple and efficient. The CoAP is intended to be used in resource-constrained devices and widely used in IoT and machine-to-machine networks.

Fig. 4.6 shows protocols that have been developed at different layers of IoT, including messaging protocols at application layer, such as CoAP, routing protocols (such as the routing protocol for low power and lossy network, RPL). In this protocol, the IPv6 is one of the most important enablers in the IoT environment that supports the possibility to connect billions of smart objectives together. However, all protocols should be designed by following the security requirements.

Communication in IoT-constrained environment

- CoAP (RFC 7252), which is designed for special requirements of constrained environments like IoT and similar to HTTP with RESTful architecture style
- DTLS binding
- User controls the device and data through authorization

4.4.1 Datagram Transport Layer Security

In the Internet, the TLS is a prominent IP-based security protocol which is widely used to provide protection over transparent connection-orient channel

- Various protocols applied to IoT networks
- Relevant protocols for different layers
  - Link layer (e.g., 802.15.4, PLC)
  - Adaption layer (6LowPAN)
  - Routing (e.g., RPL)
  - Messaging (e.g., CoAP)
  - Security: (D) TLS, 802.1AR, 802. 1X

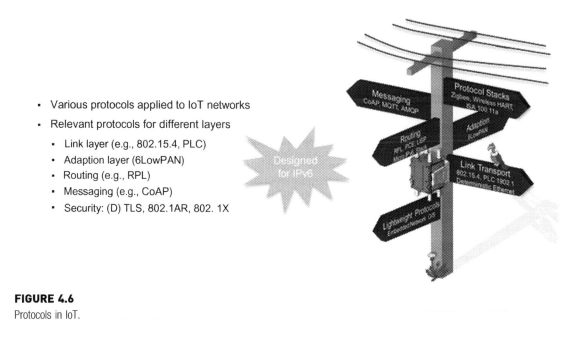

FIGURE 4.6

Protocols in IoT.

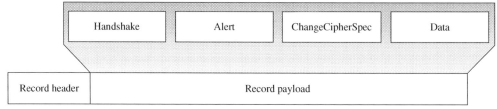

FIGURE 4.7

Structure of the DTLS.

against security attacks, such as eavesdropping, tampering, or message forgery. In web applications, the TLS is widely used for web protocols, such as HTTP and TCP. Fig. 4.7 shows the structure of DTLS.

In IoT applications, the security protocol is particularly targeted for small, low-power sensors, switches, valves, and similar components that need to be controlled or supervised remotely, through standard Internet works. The DTLS is developed based on TLS by providing equivalent security services, such as confidentiality, authentication, and integrity protection. The TLS uses the TCP and therefore does not encounter packet reordering and packet loss issues. In DTLS, a handshake mechanism is designed to deal with the packet-loss, reordering, and retransmission. In DTLS, the initial authentication of the peers and key agreement and then data protection is provided via the secure channel. In DTLS, the lower layer is the record protocol which protects all DTLS messages as shown in Fig. 4.7. The upper layer is record protocol payload; it consists of four protocol types:

- Handshake, DTLS provides three types of handshake: nonauthentication, server authentication, and server and client authentication
- Alert
- ChangeCipherSpec
- Data

Mutual certificate-based DTLS handshake. Client and server possess a pair of private–public keys. They exchange during the handshake their public keys. Each public key is bound to an identity by means of a certificate. For freshness of keying material and providing perfect forward secrecy random values and ephemeral DH key pairs are generated at each side, exchanged and incorporated into the calculation of the keying material (Fig. 4.8).

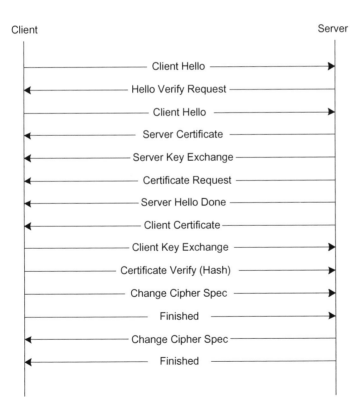

FIGURE 4.8

Mutual certificate-based DTLS handshake procedure.

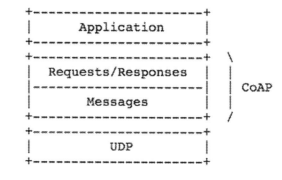

FIGURE 4.9
Structure of the CoAP.

4.4.2 Constrained Application Protocol

The CoAP is particularly designed web transfer protocol for use with resource-constrained networks and devices. It is very suitable for IoT environment, where lots of end-nodes often have only 8/16-bit microcontrollers with small amounts of ROM and RAM, while constrained network such as IPv6 over low-power Wireless Personal Area Networks (6LoWPANs) often have high packet error rates and a typical throughput of 10 s of kbps. The CoAP provides a request–response interaction model between applications. CoAP supports built-in discovery of services and resources, includes key concepts of the Web, URIs, etc. Fig. 4.9 shows the basic structure of CoAP.

CoAP defines four types of message:

- Confirmable
- Nonconfirmable
- Acknowledgment
- Reset

The basic exchange of the four types of messages are somewhat orthogonal to the request–response interactions; requests can be carried in confirmable and nonconfirmable message, and responses can be carried in these as well as piggybacked in acknowledge messages.

4.5 LIGHTWEIGHT CRYPTOGRAPHY

We propose to adopt new advancing technology, "Lightweight Cryptography," in the IoT. We described two reasons that support our proposal.

4.5.1 Efficiency of End-to-End Communication

In order to achieve end-to-end security, end-nodes have an implementation of a symmetric key algorithm. For the low resource-devices, for example, battery-powered devices, the cryptographic operation with a limited amount of energy consumption is important. Application of the lightweight symmetric key algorithm allows lower energy consumption for end devices.

4.5.2 Applicability to Lower Resource Devices

The footprint of the lightweight cryptographic primitives is smaller than the conventional cryptographic ones. The lightweight cryptographic primitives would open possibilities of more network connections with lower resource devices.

A comparison of the lightweight properties with the conventional cryptographic primitives is shown in Table 4.3. The comparison in Appendix focuses on hardware properties. Some end-nodes might be able to embed general-purpose microprocessors and software properties are considered important in such platforms. However, lowest cost devices can embed only application-specific ICs due to limited cost and power consumption, where hardware properties are crucially important.

Cryptographic technologies are advancing: new techniques on attack, design, and implementation are extensively studied. One of the state-of-the-art techniques is "Lightweight Cryptography (LWC)." Lightweight cryptography is a cryptographic algorithm or protocol tailored for implementation in constrained environments including RFID tags, sensors, contactless smart cards, healthcare devices, and so on.

The properties of lightweight cryptography have already been discussed in ISO/IEC 29192 in ISO/IEC JTC 1/SC 27. ISO/IEC 29192 is a new standardization project of lightweight cryptography, and the project is in process of standardization. In ISO/IEC 29192, lightweight properties are described based on target platforms. In hardware implementations, chip size and/or energy consumption are the important measures to evaluate the lightweight properties. In software implementations, the smaller code and/or RAM size are preferable for the lightweight applications. From the view of the implementation properties, the lightweight primitives are superior to conventional cryptographic ones, which are currently used in the Internet security protocols, for example, IPsec, TLS.

Lightweight cryptography also delivers adequate security. Lightweight cryptography does not always exploit the security-efficiency trade-offs. We report recent technologies of lightweight cryptographic primitives.

Table 4.3 Results on Hardware Performance

	Mode	Block Size (Bits)	Key Size (Bits)	Cycle	Area (GE)	Frequency (MHz)	Throughput (Mbps)	Technology (μm)
Serialized Implementation (Area Optimization)								
PRESENT	enc	64	80	547	1075	0.1	0.0117	0.18
PRESENT	enc	64	128	559	1391	0.1	0.0115	0.18
CLEFIA	enc	128	128	176	2893	67	49	0.13
CLEFIA	enc/dec	128	128	176	2996	61	44	0.13
AES	enc	128	128	177	3100	152	110	0.13
AES	enc/dec	128	128	1032	3400	80	10	0.35
Round-Based Implementation (Efficiency Optimization)								
PRESENT	enc	64	80	32	1570	0.1	0.20	0.18
PRESENT	enc	64	128	32	1884	0.1	0.20	0.18
CLEFIA	enc/dec	128	128	36	4950	201.3	715.69	0.09
CLEFIA	enc/dec	128	128	18	5979	225.8	1605.94	0.09
AES	enc/dec	128	128	11	12,454	145.4	1691.35	0.13
AES	enc/dec	128	128	54	5398	131.2	311.09	0.13

Lightweight cryptography contributes to the security of smart objects networks because of its efficiency and smaller footprint. We believe that lightweight primitives should be considered to be implemented in the networks. Especially, lightweight block ciphers are practical to use now (Table 4.3).

4.6   EXISTING SECURITY SCHEMES FOR IoT

In existing networks, a number of data protection solutions have been applied for protection of data. In IoT environment, security still is a big concern. In IoT, from the nodes to the applications, the security challenges have posed. Fig. 4.10 shows a brief architecture of an IoT systems.

The typical security scheme should be addressed throughout the node life cycle from the initial design to the operational environment.

Secure boot: It is a process involving cryptography that allows an electronic device to start executing authenticated and trusted software to operate. To implement a secure boot with the help of public-key-based signature verification, a basic procedure is as follows. It is the foundation of trust but the nodes still need protection from various run-time threats and malicious intentions.

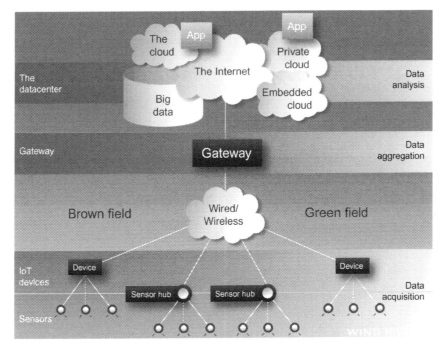

FIGURE 4.10
Structure of an IoT system.

Access control: The access control should be well designed to mandatory different forms of resources and roles in IoT. Basically, the privilege dictates that only the minimal access required to perform a function should be authorized in order to minimize the effectiveness of any breach of security.

Existing PKC schemes verify the integrity and authenticity of digital contents. As mentioned above, the integrity means that the digital content has not be been modified since it was created. Authenticity means that the same digital content has been released by a well-identified entity. The digital signature provides the two fundamental characteristics to make sure the digital content is trusted by other entity.

1. Integrity of digital content is guaranteed by message digest, that is, a secure hash algorithm (SHA-1, SHA-256, SHA-3, etc.).
2. The authenticity of digital content is guaranteed by the public-key-based signature scheme itself. PKC is based on pairs of keys. Anyone can possess a pair of keys: one private key stored secretly (K_PRIV), and one public key (K_PUB) publicly available to anyone. The K_PRIV can be used to sign digital content. The issuer of the digital content uses its own K_PRIV to identify himself/herself as the "issuer," the public key can be used by anyone to verify a digital content's signature.

a. Hash. Hashing the digital content and producing a hash value with the properties.
b. Sign. The hash value is signed (encrypt hash using K_PRIV) using the K_PRIV of the digital content author. The procedure value is called "signature" that is attached to the original digital content.
   Verify. If one wants to verify the digital content signature they have to perform following two steps:
c. Hash again. The digital content is hashed again, as in the signature generation process.
d. Reconstructed hash value is used as an input to the signature verification algorithm together with the signature attached to the digital content and the K_PUB (decrypt using signer's K_PUB) (Fig. 4.11).

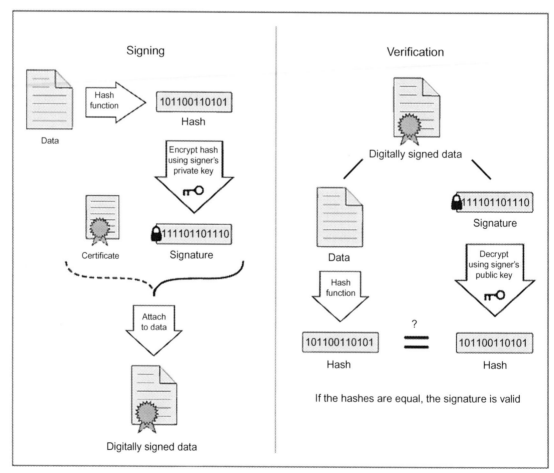

FIGURE 4.11

Example of digital sign system.

4.7 SUMMARY

The IoT is growing quickly and a number of smart objectives are bringing together, which can bring vulnerabilities in to the IoT systems and may carry serious risks for IoT devices, users, and for IoT-based applications. The hardware-based security solution can secure IoT systems and prevent damages and economic losses offering new opportunities. The IoT hardware security architecture is still in its exploratory stage, so it is facing many severe challenges than expected.

Further Reading

Fleisch, E., 2010. What is the internet of things? An economic perspective. Econom., Manage. Financ. Markets (2), 125−157.

Floerkemeier, C., Roduner, C., Lampe, M., 2007. Rfid application development with the accada middleware platform. IEEE Syst. J. 1 (2), 82−94.

Furnell, S., 2007. Making security usable: are things improving? Comput. Security 26 (6), 434−443.

Gama, K., Touseau, L., Donsez, D., 2012. Combining heterogeneous service technologies for building an internet of things middleware. Comput. Commun. 35 (4), 405−417.

Gaur, H., 2013. Internet of things: thinking services.

Gu, L., Wang, J., Sun, B., 2014. Trust management mechanism for internet of things. China Commun. 11 (2), 148−156.

He, W., Xu, L., 2012. Integration of distributed enterprise applications: a survey.

Hendricks, K.B., Singhal, V.R., Stratman, J.K., 2007. The impact of enterprise systems on corporate performance: A study of erp, scm, and crm system implementations. J. Operat. Manage. 25 (1), 65−82.

Hepp, M., Siorpaes, K., Bachlechner, D., 2007. Harvesting wiki consensus: Using wikipedia entries as vocabulary for knowledge management. IEEE Internet Comput. 11 (5), 54−65.

Hernandez-Castro, J.C., Tapiador, J.M.E., Peris-Lopez, P., Li, T., Quisquater, J.-J., 2013. Cryptanalysis of the sasi ultra-light weight rfid authentication protocol. arxiv.

Hitt, L.M., Wu, D., Zhou, X., 2002. Investment in enterprise resource planning: Business impact and productivity measures. J. Manage. Informat. Syst. 19 (1), 71−98.

Hoyland, C.A., Adams, K.M., Tolk, A., Xu, L.D., 2014. The rq-tech methodology: a new paradigm for conceptualizing strategic enterprise architectures. J. Manage. Analyt. 1 (1), 55−77.

HP Company, 2014. Internet of things research study. Retrieved from < http://digitalstrategies. tuck.dartmouth.edu/cds-uploads/people/pdf/Xu_IoTSecurity.pdf >.

ITU, 2013. The internet of things, international telecommunication union (itu) internet report.

Kang, K., Pang, Z., Da Xu, L., Ma, L., Wang, C., 2014. An interactive trust model for application market of the internet of things. IEEE Transact. Indust. Informat. 10 (2), 1516−1526.

Keoh, S., Kumar, S., Tschofenig, H., 2014. Securing the internet of things: a standardization perspective.

Kim, H., 2012. Security and vulnerability of SCADA systems over ip-based wireless sensor networks. International J. Distribut. Sensor Networks 8 (11), 268478.

Klair, D.K., Chin, K.-W., Raad, R., 2010. A survey and tutorial of rfid anti-collision protocols. IEEE Commun. Surv. Tutor. 12 (3), 400–421.

Kranenburg, R.v., Anzelmo, E., Bassi, A., Caprio, D., Dodson, S., Ratto, M., 2011. The internet of things. Paper presented at the 1st Berlin Symposium on Internet and Society (Versión electrónica). Consultado el.

Li, D.X., 2011. Enterprise systems: state-of-the-art and future trends. IEEE Transact. Indust. Informat. 7 (4), 630–640.

Li, F., Xiong, P., 2013. Practical secure communication for integrating wireless sensor networks into the internet of things.

Li, L., Li, S., Zhao, S., 2014. Qos-aware scheduling of services-oriented internet of things.

Li, L., Wang, B., Wang, A., 2014. An emergency resource allocation model for maritime chemical spill accidents. J. Manage. Analyt. 1, 146–155.

Li, S., Da Xu, L., Zhao, S., 2014. The internet of things: a survey. Informat. Syst. Front. 17, 243–259.

Lim, M.K., Bahr, W., Leung, S.C., 2013. Rfid in the warehouse: a literature analysis (1995–2010) of its applications, benefits, challenges and future trends. Int. J. Product. Econom. 145 (1), 409–430.

Miorandi, D., Sicari, S., De Pellegrini, F., Chlamtac, I., 2012. Internet of things: vision, applications and research challenges. Ad Hoc Networks 10 (7), 1497–1516.

Ning, H., 2013. Unit and Ubiquitous Internet of Things. CRC Press, Boca Raton, FL.

Ning, H., Liu, H., Yang, L.T., 2013. Cyberentity security in the internet of things. Computer 46 (4), 46–53.

Oppliger, R., 2011. Security and privacy in an online world. Computer 44 (9), 21–22.

Peris-Lopez, P., Hernandez-Castro, J.C., Estevez-Tapiador, J.M., Ribagorda, A., 2006. M2ap: a minimalist mutual-authentication protocol for low-cost rfid tags. Ubiquitous Intelligence and Computing. Springer, Heidelberg, pp. 912–923.

Perna, M., 2013. Security 101: securing SCADA environments. Retrieved from <http://blog.fortinet.com/post/security-101-securing-scada-environments>.

Pretz, K., 2013. The next evolution of the internet. Retrieved from <http://theinstitute.ieee.org/technology-focus/technology-topic/the-next-evolution-of-the-internet>.

Raza, S., Voigt, T., Jutvik, V., 2012. Lightweight ikev2: a key management solution for both the compressed ipsec and the ieee 802.15. 4 security. Paper presented at the Proceedings of the IETF Workshop on Smart Object Security.

Raza, S., Shafagh, H., Hewage, K., Hummen, R., Voigt, T., 2013. Lithe: lightweight secure coap for the internet of things.

Roe, D., 2014. Top 5 internet of things security concerns. Retrieved from <http://www.cmswire.com/cms/internet-of-things/top-5-internet-of-things-security-concerns-026043.php>.

Roman, R., Najera, P., Lopez, J., 2011. Securing the internet of things. Computer 44 (9), 51–58.

Roman, R., Zhou, J., Lopez, J., 2013. On the features and challenges of security and privacy in distributed internet of things. Comput. Networks 57 (10), 2266–2279.

Sundmaeker, H., Guillemin, P., Friess, P., Woelfflé, S., 2010. Vision and challenges for realising the internet of things: EUR-OP.

Tan, W., Chen, S., Li, J., Li, L., Wang, T., Hu, X., 2014. A trust evaluation model for e-learning systems. Syst. Res. Behav. Sci. 31 (3), 353–365.

Tao, F., Cheng, Y., Xu, L.D., Zhang, L., Li, B.H., 2014. Cciot-cmfg: cloud computing and internet of things based cloud manufacturing service system.

Wang, F., Ge, B., Zhang, L., Chen, Y., Xin, Y., Li, X., 2013. A system framework of security management in enterprise systems. Syst. Res. Behav. Sci. 30 (3), 287–299.

Wang, K., Wu, M., 2010. Cooperative communications based on trust model for mobile ad hoc networks. IET Informat. Security 4 (2), 68–79.

Weber, R.H., 2013. Internet of things–governance quo vadis? Comput. Law Security Rev. 29 (4), 341–347.

Welbourne, E., Battle, L., Cole, G., Gould, K., Rector, K., Raymer, S., et al., 2009. Building the internet of things using rfid: the rfid ecosystem experience. IEEE Internet Comput. 13 (3), 48–55.

Wieder, B., Booth, P., Matolcsy, Z.P., Ossimitz, M.-L., 2006. The impact of erp systems on firm and business process performance. J. Enterprise Informat. Manage. 19 (1), 13–29.

Xiao, G., Guo, J., Xu, L., Gong, Z., 2014. User interoperability with heterogeneous iot devices through transformation.

Xu, B., Xu, L.D., Cai, H., Xie, C., Hu, J., Bu, F., 2014. Ubiquitous data accessing method in iot-based information system for emergency medical services.

Xu, L., He, W., Li, S., 2014. Internet of things in industries: a survey. IEEE Transact. Indust. Informat. 99, 1.

Xu, L.D., 2011. Information architecture for supply chain quality management. Int. J. Product. Res. 49 (1), 183–198.

Yao, X., Han, X., Du, X., Zhou, X., 2013. A lightweight multicast authentication mechanism for small scale iot applications.

Yuan Jie, F., Yue Hong, Y., Li Da, X., Yan, Z., Fan, W., 2014. Iot-based smart rehabilitation system. IEEE Transact. Indust. Informat. 10 (2), 1568–1577.

CHAPTER 5

Security Requirements in IoT Architecture

Shancang Li

5.1 INTRODUCTION

A critical requirement of IoT is that the devices must be interconnected, which makes it to be able to perform specific tasks, such as sensing, communicating, information processing, etc. The IoT is able to acquire, transmit, and process the information from the IoT end-nodes (such as RFID devices, sensors, gateway, intelligent devices, etc.) via network to accomplish highly complex tasks. The IoT should be able to provide applications with strong security protection (e.g., for online payment application, the IoT should be able to protect the integrity of payment information) (Fig. 5.1).

The system architecture must provide operational guarantees for the IoT, which bridges the gap between the physical devices and the virtual worlds. In designing the framework of IoT, following factors should be taken into consideration: (1) technical factors, such as sensing techniques, communication methods, network technologies, etc.; (2) security protection, such as information confidentiality, transmission security, privacy protection, etc.; (3) business issues, such as business models, business processes, etc. Currently, the service-oriented architecture (SoA) has been successfully applied to IoT design, where the applications are moving towards service-oriented integration technologies. In business domain, the complex applications among diverse services have been appearing. Services reside in different layers of the IoT such as: sensing layer, network layer, services layer, and application−interface layer. The services-based application will heavily depend on the architecture of IoT. Fig. 5.2 depicts a generic SoA for IoT, which consists of four layers:

- *Sensing layer* is integrated with end components of IoT to sense and acquire the information of devices;
- *Network layer* is the infrastructure to support wireless or wired connections among things;

Securing the Internet of Things. DOI: http://dx.doi.org/10.1016/B978-0-12-804458-2.00005-6
© 2017 Elsevier Inc. All rights reserved.

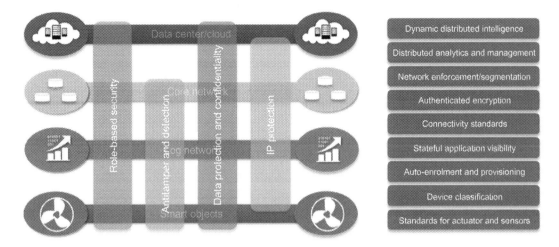

FIGURE 5.1
Security framework in the IoT environment.

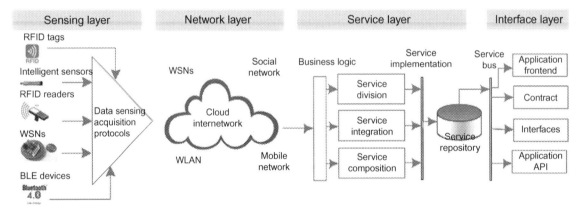

FIGURE 5.2
SoA for IoT (Bi et al., 2014).

- *Service layer* is to provide and manage services required by users or applications;
- *Application—interfaces layer* consists of interaction methods with users or applications.

The security requirements on each layer might be different due to its features. In general, the security solution for the IoT considers following requirements:

1. Sensing layer and IoT end-node security requirements,
2. Network layer security requirements,
3. Service layer security requirements,

4. Application–interface layer security requirements,
5. The security requirements between layers, and
6. Security requirements for services running and maintenance.

5.1.1 Security Challenges in IoT Environment

In IoT systems, most of the smart things are typically small, inexpensive, with limited security capabilities. The existing advanced cryptographic algorithms are unable to process since the low CPU cycles and low effective encryption.

There are seemingly competing, complex security requirements to be deployed on a platform with potentially limited resources:

- Authenticate to multiple networks securely
- Ensure that data are available to multiple collectors
- Manage the contention between the data access
- Manage privacy concerns between multiple consumers
- Provide strong authentication and data protection (integrity and confidentiality) that are not easily compromised
- Maintain availability of the data or the service
- Allow for evolution in the face of unknown risks

Fig. 5.3 shows a framework to secure the devices in IoT.

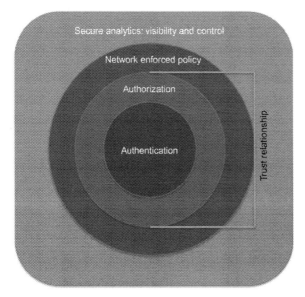

FIGURE 5.3
Security architecture for IoT.

5.1.2   Sensing Layer and IoT End-Nodes

The IoT is a multilayer network that interconnects devices for information acquisition, exchange, and processing. At the sensing layer, the intelligent tags and sensor networks are able to automatically sense the environment and exchange data among devices (Li, 2011). In determining the sensing layer of an IoT, the main concerns are:

- *Cost*, *size*, *resource*, and *energy consumption*. The things might be equipped with sensing devices such as RFID tags, sensors, actuator, etc., which should be designed to minimize required resources as well as cost.
- *Deployment*. The IoT end-nodes (such as RFID reader, tags, sensors, etc.) can be deployed one-time, or in incremental or random ways depending on application requirements.
- *Heterogeneity*. A variety of things or hybrid networks make the IoT very heterogeneous.
- *Communication*. The IoT end-nodes should be designed able to communicate each other.
- *Networks*. The IoT involves hybrid networks, such as wireless sensor networks, Wireless Mesh Networks (WMNs), and supervisory control and data acquisition systems.

The security is an important concern in sensing layer. It is expected that IoT could be connected with industrial networks to provide users smart services. However, it may cause new concerns in controlling the devices, such as who can input authentication credentials or decide whether an application should be trusted. The security model in IoT must be able to make its own judgments and decision about whether to accept a command or execute a task. At sensing layer, the devices are designed for low power consumption with constraints resources, which often have limited connectivity. The endless variety of IoT applications poses an equally wide variety of security challenges.

- Devices authentication
- Trusted devices
- Leveraging the security controls and availability of infrastructures in sensing layer
- Cryptoresilience and cryptoalgorithms have a limited lifetime before IoT devices
- Physical protection
- Tamper detection techniques

In terms of software update, how the sensing devices receive software updates or security patches in a timely manner without impairing functional safety or incurring significant recertification costs every time a patch is rolled out.

In this layer, the security concerns can be classified into two main categories:

- The security requirements at IoT end-node: physical security protection, access control, authentication, nonrepudiation, confidentiality, integrity, availability, and privacy.
- The security requirements in sensing layer: confidentiality, data source authentication, device authentication, integrity, availability, and timeless.

Table 5.1 summarizes the potential security threats and security vulnerabilities at IoT end-node and Table 5.2 analyzes the security threats and vulnerabilities in sensing layer.

As mentioned above, in this layer, most devices are typically small in size, inexpensive, and with little to physical security. These devices could be in remote and/or inaccessible locations but may not support complex and evolving security algorithms due to limited resources. At these nodes, methods must be taken to ensure that the authenticity of the data/user,

Table 5.1 Security Threats and Vulnerabilities at IoT End-Node

Security Threats	Description
Unauthorized access	Due to physical capture or logic attacked, the sensitive information at the end-nodes is captured by the attacker
Availability	The end-node stops to work since physically captured or attacked logically
Spoofing attack	With malware node, the attacker successfully masquerades as IoT end-device, end-node, or end-gateway by falsifying data
Selfish threat	Some IoT end-nodes stop working to save resources or bandwidth to cause the failure of network
Malicious code	Virus, Trojan, and junk message that can cause software failure
Denial of Services (DoS)	An attempt to make an IoT end-node resource unavailable to its users
Transmission threats	Threats in transmission, such as interrupting, blocking, data manipulation, forgery, etc.
Routing attack	Attacks on a routing path

Table 5.2 Analysis of the Security Threats and Vulnerabilities in Sensing Layer

IoT End-Node Threats and Vulnerabilities	IoT End-Devices	IoT End-Node	IoT End-Gateway
Unauthorized access	√	√	√
Selfish threat		√	√
Spoofing attack		√	√
Malicious code	√	√	√
DoS	√	√	√
Transmission threats			√
Routing attack	√	√	√

the access control of the devices, and the connectivity authentication parameters between the initial configuration and its presence in run-time at IoT environment cannot be compromised.

Specifically, to secure devices in this layer before users are at risk, following actions should be taken: (1) Implement security standards for IoT and ensure all devices are produced by meeting specific security standards; (2) Build trustworthy data sensing system and review the security of all devices/components; (3) Forensically identify and trace the source of users; (4) Software or firmware at IoT end-node should be securely designed.

5.2 NETWORK LAYER

The network layer connects all things in IoT and allows them to be aware of their surroundings. It is capable of aggregating data from existing IT infrastructures and then transmits to other layers, such as sensing layer, service layers, etc. The IoT connects a variety of different networks, which may cause a lot of difficulties on network problems, security problems, and communication problems.

The deployment, management, and scheduling of networks are essential for the network layer in IoT. This enables devices to perform tasks collaboratively. In the networking layer, the following issues should be addressed:

- Network management technologies including the management for fixed, wireless, mobile networks
- Network energy efficiency
- Requirements of QoS
- Technologies for mining and searching
- Information confidentiality
- Security and privacy

Among these issues, information confidentiality and human privacy security are critical because of its deployment, mobility, and complexity. The existing network security technologies can provide a basis for privacy and security protection in IoT, but more works are still needed to be done. The security requirements in network layer involve:

- *Overall security requirements*, including confidentiality, integrity, privacy protection, authentication, group authentication, keys protection, availability, etc.
- *Privacy leakage*. Since some IoT devices are physically located in untrusted places, which cause potential risks for attackers to physically find the privacy information such as user identification, etc.
- *Communication security*. It involves the integrity and confidentiality of signaling in IoT communications.

- *Overconnected*. The overconnected IoT may run risk of losing control of the user. Two security concerns may be caused: (1) DoS attack, the bandwidth required by signaling authentication can cause network congestion and further cause DoS; (2) Keys security, for the overconnected network, the keys operations could cause heavy network resources consumption.
- *MITM attack*, the attacker makes independent connections with the victims and relays messages between them, making them believe that they are talking directly to each other over a private connection, when in fact the attacker controls the entire conversation.
- *Fake network message*, attackers could create fake signaling to isolate/misoperate the devices from the IoT.
- *Confidential compromise*, the data in network are being relayed and can be altered by an attacker.
- *Relay attack*, the valid data could be retransmitted or delayed by an adversary to gain access to an already established connection by spoofing their own identity.

In the network layer, the possible security threats are summarized in Tables 5.3 and 5.4, the potential security threats and vulnerabilities are analyzed.

Table 5.3 Security Threats in Network Layer

Security Threats	Description
Data breach	Information release of secure information to an untrusted environment
DoS	An attempt to make an IoT end-node resource unavailable to its users
Public key and private key	The comprise of keys in networks
Malicious code	Virus, Trojan, and junk message that can cause software failure
Transmission threats	Threats in transmission, such as interrupting, blocking, data manipulation, forgery, etc.
Routing attack	Attacks on a routing path

Table 5.4 The Security Threats and Vulnerabilities in Network Layer

	Privacy Leakage	Confidentiality	Integrity	DoS	PKI	MITM	Request Forgery
Physical protection	√	√					√
Transmission security		√	√	√	√	√	√
Overconnected			√	√	√		
Cross-layer fusion	√	√				√	√

The network infrastructure and protocols developed for IoT are different with existing IP network; special efforts are needed on following security concerns: (1) Authentication/Authorization, which involves vulnerabilities such as password, access control, etc. and (2) Secure transport encryption, it is crucial to encrypt the transmission in this layer.

5.3 SERVICE LAYER

In IoT, the service layer relies on middleware technology, which is an important enabler of services and applications. The service layer provides IoT a cost-effective platform where the hardware and software platforms could be reused. The IoT illustrates the activities required by the middle service specifications, which are undertaken by various standards developed by the service providers and organizations. The service layer is designed based on the common requirements of applications, application programming interfaces (APIs), and service protocols. The core set of services in this layer might include following components: event processing service, integration services, analytics services, UI services, and security and management services (Choi et al., 2012). The activities in service layer, such as information exchange, data processing, ontologies databases, communications between services, are conducted by following components:

- *Service discovery.* It finds that infrastructure can provide the required service and information in an effective way.
- *Service composition.* It enables the combination and interaction among connected things. Discovery exploits the relationships of things to find the desired service, and service composition schedules or recreates more suitable services to obtain the most reliable ones.
- *Trustworthiness management.* It aims at understanding how the trusted devices and information are provided by other services.
- *Service APIs.* It provides the interactions between services required by users.

Recently, a number of service layer solutions have been reported. The SOCRADES integration architecture is proposed that can be used to interact between applications and service layers effectively (Fielding and Taylor, 2002); things are abstracted as devices to provide services at low levels as network discovery services, metadata exchange services, and asynchronous publish and subscribe event (Kranenburg et al., 2011; Sundmaeker et al., 2010); In Peris-Lopez et al. (2006), a representational state transfer is defined to increase interoperability between loosely coupled services and distributed applications. In Hernandez-Castro et al. (2013), the services layer introduced a service provisioning process that can provide the interaction between applications and services. It is important to design an effective security strategy to protect services against attacks in the service layer. The security requirements in the service layer include:

- Authorization, service authentication, group authentication, privacy protection, integrity, integrity, security of keys, nonrepudiation, antireplay, availability, etc.
- Privacy leakage. The main concern in this layer involves privacy leakage and malicious location tracking.
- Service abuses, in IoT the service abuse attack involves: (i) illegal abuse of services; (ii) abuse of unsubscribed services.
- Node identify masquerade.
- DoS attack.
- Replay attack, the attacker resends the data.
- Service information sniffer and manipulation.
- Repudiation in service layer includes the communication repudiation and services repudiation.

The security solution should be able to protect the operations on this layer from potential threats. Table 5.5 summarizes the security threats on the service layer.

The data security in services layer is crucial and more complicate. It involves fragmented, full of competing standards and proprietary solutions. The SoA is very helpful to improve the security of this layer, but following challenges still need to be faced when building an IoT services or application: (1) data transmission security between service and/or layers; (2) secure services management, such as service identification, access control, services composite, etc.

Table 5.5 The Security Threats in Service Layer

Security Threats	Description
Privacy threats	Privacy leakage or malicious location tracking
Services abuse	Unauthorized users access services or the authorized users access unsubscribed services
Identity masquerade	The IoT end-device, node, or gateway are masqueraded by attacker
Service information manipulation	The information in services is manipulated by the attacker
Repudiation	Denial of the operations have been done
DoS	An attempt to make an IoT end-node resource unavailable to its users
Replay attack	The attack resends the information to spoof the receiver
Routing attack	Attacks on a routing path

5.4   APPLICATION−INTERFACE LAYER

The application−interface layer involves a variety of applications and interfaces from RFID tag tracking to smart home, which are implemented by standard protocols as well as service-composition technologies (Ning, 2013). The requirements in application−interface layer strongly depend on the applications. For the application maintenance, following security requirements will be involved:

- Remote safe configuration, software downloading and updating, security patches, administrator authentication, unified security platform, etc.For the security requirements on communications between layers:
- Integrity and confidentiality for transmission between layers, cross-layer authentication and authorization, sensitive information isolation, etc. In IoT designing for the security solutions, following rules should be helpful:
  a. Since most constrained IoT end-node works in an unattended manner, the designer should pay more attention to the safety of these nodes;
  b. Since IoT involves billions of clustering nodes, the security solutions should be designed based on energy efficiency schemes;
  c. The light security scheme at IoT end-nodes might be different with existing network security solutions; however, we should design security solutions in a big enough range for all parts in IoT.

Table 5.6 summarizes the security threats and vulnerabilities in IoT application−interface layer.

In Table 5.7, we analyze the security threats and potential vulnerabilities in application−interface layer.

Table 5.6 The Security Threats in Application−Interface Layer

Security Threats	Description
Remote configuration	Fail to configure at interfaces
Misconfiguration	Misconfiguration at remote IoT end-node, end-device, or end-gateway
Security management	Log and keys leakage
Management system	Failure of management system

Table 5.7 The Security Threats and Vulnerabilities in Application—Interface Layer

	Unauthorized Access	Failure of Node	Masquerade	Selfish Node	Trojan, Virus, Spam	Privacy Leakage
Physical security protection	√	√	√			
Antivirus, firewalling				√		
Access control	√	√	√			√
Confidential	√	√	√			√
Data integrity		√	√	√	√	
Availability						
Authentication	√	√	√			√
Nonrepudiation	√	√	√			√

Table 5.8 Security Threats Between Layers in the IoT Architecture

Security Threats	Description
Sensitive information leakage at border	The sensitive information might be not protected at the border of layers
Identity spoofing	The identities in different layers have different priorities
Sensitive information spreads between layers	Sensitive information spreads at different layers and cause information leakage

The application—interface layer bridges the IoT system with user applications, which should be able to ensure that the interaction of IoT systems with other applications or users are legal and can be trusted.

5.5 CROSS-LAYER THREATS

Information in the IoT architecture might be shared among all of the four layers to achieve full interoperability between services and devices. It brings a number of security challenges such as trust guarantee, privacy of the users and their data, secure data sharing among layers, etc. In the IoT architecture described in Fig. 5.1, information is exchanged between different layers, which may cause potential threats as shown in Table 5.8.

The security requirements in this layer include (1) security protection, securing to be ensured at design and execution time; (2) privacy protection, personal information access within IoT system, privacy standards and enhancement technologies; (3) trust has to be a part of IoT architecture and must be built in.

Table 5.9 Security Threats Between Layers in the IoT Architecture

Security Threats	Description
Remote configuration	Fail to configure remote IoT end-node, end-device, or end-gateway
Misconfiguration	Misconfiguration at remote IoT end-node, end-device, or end-gateway
Security management	Log and keys leakage at IoT end-node
Management system	Failure of management system

5.6 THREATS CAUSED IN MAINTENANCE OF IoT

The maintenance of IoT can cause security problems, such as in configuration of the network, security management, and application managements. Table 5.9 summarized the potential threats that can cause risky in IoT.

References

Bi, Z., Xu, L., Wang, C., 2014. Internet of things for enterprise systems of modern manufacturing. Ind. Inf., IEEE Trans. 10 (2), 1537−1546.

Choi, J., Li, S., Wang, X., Ha, J., 2012. A general distributed consensus algorithm for wireless sensor networks. Wireless Advanced (WiAd), 2012. IEEE, London, United Kingdom, pp. 16−21.

Fielding, R.T., Taylor, R.N., 2002. Principled design of the modern web architecture. ACM Trans. Internet Technol. (TOIT) 2 (2), 115−150.

Hernandez-Castro, J.C., Tapiador, J.M.E., Peris-Lopez, P., Li, T., and Quisquater, J.-J. (2013). Cryptanalysis of the SASI ultralightweight RFID authentication protocol. ArXiv.

Li, D.X., 2011. Enterprise systems: State-of-the-art and future trends. Ind. Inf., IEEE Trans. 7 (4), 630−640.

Ning, H., 2013. Unit and Ubiquitous Internet of Things. CRC Press.

Peris-Lopez, P., Hernandez-Castro, J.C., Estevez-Tapiador, J.M., Ribagorda, A., 2006. M^2AP: a minimalist mutual-authentication protocol for low-cost rfid tags. Ubiquitous Intelligence and Computing. Springer-Verlag, Berlin, Heidelberg, pp. 912−923.

Sundmaeker, H., Guillemin, P., Friess, P., Woelfflé, S., 2010. Vision and Challenges for Realising the Internet of Things. EUR-OP.

CHAPTER 6

Security in Enabling Technologies

Shancang Li and Li Da Xu

6.1 SECURITY IN IDENTIFICATION AND TRACKING TECHNOLOGIES

The concept of IoT was coined based on the radio-frequency identification (RFID)-enabled identification and tracking technologies. A basic RFID system consists of an RFID reader and RFID tags. Due to its capability for identifying, tracing, and tracking, the RFID system has been widely applied in logistics, such as package tracking, supply chain management, healthcare applications, etc. An RFID system could provide sufficient real-time information about things in IoT, which are very useful to manufacturers, distributors, and retailers. For example, RFID application in supply chain management can improve backroom inventory-management practices.

Although RFID technology is successfully used in many areas, it is still evolving in developing active system, Inkjet-printing-based RFID, and management technologies (Hepp et al., 2007). For adoption by IoT, more identified problems need to be resolved, such as: *collision of RFID readings*, *signal interferences*, *privacy protection*, *standardization*, *integration*, etc.

In the new era of IoT, the scope of identifications has expended and included RFIDs, barcodes, and other intelligent sensing technologies. In RFID-enabled contactless technologies (ISO 14443 and 15693), security features have been implemented, such as cryptographic challenge–response authentication, 128-bit AES, triple-DES, and SHA-2 algorithms. The increasing use of RFID devices requires RFID security guarantee from multiple sides: manufacture, privacy protection, and business processes. In general, the security features of RFID include:

- Tags/Readers collision problem
- Data confidentiality

Securing the Internet of Things. DOI: http://dx.doi.org/10.1016/B978-0-12-804458-2.00006-8
© 2017 Elsevier Inc. All rights reserved.

Table 6.1 Security Features in RFID Standards			
Security RFID\	Confidentiality	Integrity	Availability
EPC Class 0/0+		√	√
EPC Class 1 G1		√	√
EPC Class 1 G2	√	√	√
ISO/IEC 18000-2	√	√	
ISO/IEC 18000-3	√	√	√
ISO/IEC 11784/5	√	√	
ISO/IEC 15693	√	√	√
Nonrepudiation	√	√	√

- Tag-to-reader authentication
- High-assurance readers

Table 6.1 summarizes the security features of RFID standards.

In RFID technologies, the security and privacy protection are not just technical issues; important policy questions arise as RFID tags join to create large sensor networks.

6.1.1 Identification

6.1.1.1 Tracking

In the location-based service in IoT, the exact location is commonly used; however in security viewpoint, it is potential to eliminate privacy. The attacker may spy on people in exchange for services with IoT. Security vulnerabilities are widespread in most IoT devices, which make the IoT vulnerable to attackers. The surveillance-related side of IoT is being put to use in a very open and even beneficial manner. GPS sensors can be easily placed in a smart device, for example, in smart shoes of elders, so that people can surveil them to ensure they don't wander off or go to unsafe place. However, in many cases, the devices have to hide itself for avoiding being spy or attack. The common ways to make sure devices aren't tracking are:

- Switch off "discoverable" Bluetooth to make sure the MAC address is unable to be identified.
- WiFi: similar to Bluetooth, the WiFi connected device can be identified according to the signal strength.
- GPS-related functions on the IoT devices can be used to pinpoint the location without your consent.
- Privacy app or stealth device, secure privacy add-ones, know your rights.

6.2 SECURITY IN INTEGRATION OF WIRELESS SENSOR NETWORK AND RFID

The integration of wireless sensors and RFID empowers IoT in the implementation of industrial services and the further deployment of services in extended applications. IoT with the integration of RIFD and wireless sensor networks (WSNs) makes it possible to develop IoT applications for healthcare, decision-making of complex systems, and smart civic systems such as smart transport, cities, or water supply systems.

The security issues in integration of RFID and WSNs involve following challenges:

- *Privacy*: it involves the privacy of RFID devices and WSNs devices.
- Identification and authentication: the identification has to be protected from tracking by unauthorized user in the network.
- *Communication security*: the communication between RFID devices and IoT devices poses security threats, which need to be addressed proactively, and appropriate measures must be implemented well.
- *Trust and ownership*: trust implies the authenticity and integrity of the communication parts such as sensor nodes and RFID tags.
- *Integration.*
- *User authentication.*

RFID is increasingly used in many applications such as surveillance, credit cards, service applications, etc., which opens up a new frontier for data threats over RFID. RFID tags are typically small, less powerful, and inexpensive. RFID readers emit powerful electromagnetic fields and "red" tag data. In RFID system, the security is defined from three aspects:

- Controlled access to the information, only authorized users/devices can access (read/write).
- Control over access to the system, only authorized entities can configure/modify to the systems, all RFID-devices in the system are authentic and trustworthy.
- Confidence and trust in the system, users/services share a general perception that the system is safe and secure.

In an RFID system, the security should be guaranteed from three factors (Tag reader), which is the communication crossroads and it should be able to provide data protection in both directions:

- Back-end communication: tag readers convey data via IP communication, the key threats for the back-end communication is unauthorized access to the back server via IP networks. Fortunately, the existing sophisticated security solutions can be used to bear on the security challenges.

■ Front-end communication (RF): tag readers provide and collect data to and from tags via low-power RF communications. The security challenges between tags and readers include unauthorized access to tags, rogue and clone tags, side channel attacks, etc. It is the weakest link in most RFID systems.

In more recent RFID (Generation), Energy Performance Certificate (EPC) Generation 3 protocol is expected to provide more security guarantee to RF front-end communication to ensure broader use of RFID technologies. To enhance security in an RFID system, following possible techniques might be important:

■ Lightweight encryption: the lightweight encryption/decryption algorithms make it possible to increase the difficulties to steal data in RFID systems.
■ Tag passwords: the PINs or password could be used to verify the access of tags.
■ Tag pseudonyms, use pseudonyms: RFID tags don't have to be programmed with passwords, but change serial numbers each time they are read, this would make unauthorized tag tracking more difficult but would introduce issues of pseudonym management.

The RFID systems are widely used in our life, however more and more security cases have been reported recently. In the next generation of EPCglobal protocol will lead the way to greater data RFID security and the new security threats for RFID systems should be investigated. The latest RFID security challenges include:

■ RFID virus: it has been reported that RFID systems were vulnerable to viruses since Tags could be compromised and infected with viruses by hackers; however, a well-designed RFID implementation would eliminate the risk entirely.
■ Mobile side channel attack.
■ ExxonMobil SpeedPass Hack.

The WSN is one of the most important enabling techniques in IoT environment, which shows great promise for various IoT applications. However, the WSNs are also facing many security threats and issues. Most of them are similar to their wired counterparts while some are new. Here we summarized the attacks in WSNs as:

■ DoS
■ Attacks on information in transit
■ Sybil Attack
■ Blackhole/sinkhole attack
■ Hello flood attack
■ Wormhole attack

Fortunately, a number of security schemes have been proposed to protect information in WSNs (https://arxiv.org/ftp/arxiv/papers/0712/0712.4169.pdf) (Table 6.2).

Table 6.2 Security Schemes to Protect Information in WSNs

Security Schemes	Attacks Deterred	Network Architecture	Major Features
JAM	DoS attack (jamming)	Traditional WSN	Avoidance of jammed region by using coalesced neighbor nodes
Wormhole based	DoS attack (jamming)	Hybrid (mainly wireless partly wired) sensor network	Uses wormholes to avoid jamming
Statistical En-Route Filtering	Information spoofing	Large number of sensors, highly dense WSN	Detects and drops false reports during forwarding process
Radio Resource Testing, Random Key Predistribution etc.	Sybil attack	Traditional WSN	Uses radio resource, random key predistribution, registration procedure, position verification, and code attestation for detecting Sybil entity
Bidirectional verification multipath multibase station routing	Hello Flood attack	Traditional WSN	Adopts probabilistic secret sharing, uses bidirectional verification and multipath multibase station routing
On Communication Security	Information or data spoofing	Traditional WSN	Efficient resource management, protects the network even if part of the network is compromised
TIK	Wormhole attack, information of data spoofing	Traditional WSN	Based on symmetric cryptography, requires accurate time synchronization between all communicating parties, implements temporal leashes
Random Key Predistribution	Data and information spoofing, attacks on information in transit	Traditional WSN	Provide resilience of the network, protect the network even if part of the network is compromised, provide authentication measures for sensor nodes
	Data and information spoofing	Distributed sensor network, large-scale WSN with dynamic nature	Suitable for large WSN which allows addition and deletion of sensors, resilient to sensor node capture
REWARD	Blackhole attacks	Traditional WSN	Uses geographic routing, takes advantage of the broadcast interradio behavior to watch neighboring transmissions and detect blackhole attacks
TinySec	Data and information spoofing, message replay attack	Traditional WSN	Focuses on providing message authenticity, integrity, and confidentiality; works in the link layer
SNEP and μ TESLA	Data and information spoofing, message replay attacks	Traditional WSN	Semantic security, data authentication, replay protection, weak freshness, low communication overhead

6.3   SECURITY IN COMMUNICATIONS

In IoT things are connected together in network access layer through different communication technologies. The IoT can be seen as an aggregation of heterogeneous networks, such as WSNs, wireless mesh networks, mobile networks, RFID systems, and WLAN. The communications between things/networks are essential to make reliable information exchange, which requires the IoT to provide secure, reliable, and scalable connections. IoT would also greatly benefit from the existing communication protocols in Internet such as IPv6, as this addresses any number of things needed through the Internet directly (Pretz, 2013). The basic principles of secure communications in IoT include: *authentication, availability, confidentiality,* and *integrity*. The limit of resources of things makes it difficult to build a secure enough for IoT; however, the IoT communication systems have to be designed to provide "secure enough" by finding the right balance between effort and benefit of protection measures. The security solution for communications should be designed high enough to force the hackers give up before they succeed. The commonly used communication protocols and the potential security features include:

- RFID (e.g., ISO 18000 6c EPC class 1 Gen2): the security features include confidentiality, integrity, and availability. The security features for different standards can be found in Table 6.3.
- NFC, IEEE 802.11 (WLAN), IEEE 802.15.4, IEEE 802.15.1 (Bluetooth): in these wireless communication technologies, following security are needed: confidentiality, integrity, authentication, availability, and detection of malicious intrusion.
- IETF Low-power Wireless Personal Area Networks (6LoWPAN): since 6LoWPAN is a combination of IEEE 802.15.4 and IPv6, which may cause potential vulnerabilities from the two sides that target all layers of the stack.
- Machine-to-Machine (M2M): traditional disruptive attacks in M2M such as DoS could have new consequences in M2M.

Table 6.3 Security Features in 6LoWPAN

Layers	Main Potential Attacks
Application layer	Overwhelm attack, path-based DoS attack
Transport layer	Flooding attack
Network layer	Malicious node attack; Sybil attack; Wormhole attack, spoofing attack, routing attack, etc.
Adaption layer	Packets fragmentation attack
Link layer	Exhaustion attack, collision attack; interrogation attack
Physical layer	Tampering attack, etc.

- Traditional IP technologies, such as IP, IPv6, etc.: IPv4, secure every device, addresses nearing exhaustion, networks simply won't have enough addresses to assign to the explosion of devices unless they transit to IPv6. However, for IPv6 it could have further vulnerabilities that haven't been discovered. In IPv6, IPsec could provide authenticity and integrity with authentication header, and the encapsulated security payload provides confidentiality. Recently, the transport layer security (TLS) is developed as an alternative to IPsec to provide mutual authentication of two parties using public key infrastructures and X.509 certificates (Tao et al., 2014).
- Key Management in IoT: Many key management systems (KMSs) have been proposed in recent times. In IoT, the KMS should be designed based on standard protocols. The IPsec applies the Internet Key Exchange (IKE) for automatic key management. For IEEE 802.15.4, no KMS is defined but in Cai et al. (2014), a lightweight key management IKEv2 is proposed for 6LoWPAN IPsec and IEEE 802.15.4.

6.4 SECURITY PROTOCOLS AND PRIVACY ISSUES INTO 6LoWPAN STACK

The IoT is a hybrid network that involves a lot of heterogeneous networks, which requires multifaceted security solutions against network intrusions and disruptions. The IoT contains networks that connected with daily used devices, such as smartphones, surveillance cameras, home appliances, etc. Support for heterogeneous networks can help IoT to connect the devices with different communication specification, QoS requirements, functionalities, and goals. On the other hand, support for heterogeneity can reduce the cost to implement IoT by well integrating diversified things. Meanwhile, some of the existing networking technologies, such as architecture, protocols, network management, security schemes, can be directly applicable in an IoT context. The networks involved in IoT are core parts of security working, and each subnetwork is required to provide confidentiality, secure communication, encryption certificates, and that sort of things. In IoT no IDS and IPS are specifically designed yet, but many watchdog-based IDS and IPSs could be used in the context of IoT.

6.5 SECURITY IN SERVICE MANAGEMENT

Service management refers to the implementation and management of the services that meet the needs of users or applications. Security solution at service layer is designed specifically in the context of the services. For services such as consumer applications, logistical, surveillance, intelligent healthcare, the security concerns have some similarities: authentication, access control, privacy, integrity of information, certificates and PKI certificates, digital signature, and nonrepudiation. For different services, the security concerns might be specifically designed depending on the service feature, scenarios, and special requirements.

References

Cai, H., Xu, L., Xu, B., Xie, C., Qin, S., Jiang, L., 2014. Iot-based configurable information service platform for product lifecycle management. IEEE Trans. Ind. Infor 10 (2), 1558−1567.

Pretz, K., 2013. The next evolution of the internet. Retrieved from: < http://theinstitute.ieee.org/technology-focus/technology-topic/the-next-evolution-of-the-internet > .

Tao, F., Cheng, Y., Xu, L.D., Zhang, L., Li, B.H., 2014. CCIoT-CMfg: cloud computing and internet of things based cloud manufacturing service system. IEEE Trans. Ind. Infor. 10 (2), 1435−1442.

Further Reading

Akyildiz, I.F., Su, W., Sankarasubramaniam, Y., Cayirci, E., 2002. Wireless sensor networks: a survey. Comput. Networks 38, 393−422.

Avancha, S., 2005. A Holistic Approach to Secure Sensor Networks, PhD Dissertation, University of Maryland.

Blackert, W.J., Gregg, D.M., Castner, A.K., Kyle, E.M., Hom, R.L., Jokerst, R.M., 2003. Analyzing interaction between distributed denial of service attacks and mitigation technologies. Proceedings of the DARPA Information Survivability Conference and Exposition, vol. 1, 22−24 April 2003, pp. 26−36.

Cagalj, M., Capkun, S., Hubaux, J-P., Wormhole-based anti-jamming techniques in sensor networks. <http://lcawww.epfl.ch/Publications/Cagalj/CagaljCH05-worm.pdf>.

Chan, H, Perrig, A., Song, D., 2003. Random key predistribution schemes for sensor networks. In: IEEE Symposium on Security and Privacy, Berkeley, California, 11−14 May 2003, pp. 197−213.

Cisco IBSG projections, UN Economic & Social Affairs http://www.un.org/esa/population/publications/longrange2/WorldPop2300final.pdf.

Computerworld, 2010. Siemens: Stuxnet worm hit industrial systems, September 16, 2010.

Culler, D.E., Hong, W., 2004. Wireless sensor networks. Commun. ACM 47 (6), 30−33.

Culpepper, B.J. Tseng, H.C., 2004. Sinkhole intrusion indicators in DSR MANETs. Proceedings of the First International Conference on Broad Band Networks, pp. 681−688.

Dai, S, Jing, X, Li, L, 2005. Research and analysis on routing protocols for wireless sensor networks. Proceedings of the International Conference on Communications, Circuits and Systems, vol. 1, 27−30 May 2005, pp. 407−411.

Delay Tolerant Networking Research Group. <http://www.dtnrg.org/wiki>.

Douceur, J., 2002. The Sybil Attack, 1st International Workshop on Peer-to-Peer Systems.

Du, W., Deng, J., Han, Y.S., Varshney, P.K., 2003. A pairwise key pre-distribution scheme for wireless sensor networks. Proceedings of the 10th ACM Conference on Computer and Communications Security, pp. 42−51.

Duqu: a Stuxnet-like malware found in the wild, technical report. October 14, 2011, Laboratory of Cryptography of Systems Security.

Eschenauer, L. Gligor, V.D., 2002. A key-management scheme for distributed sensor networks. Proceedings of the ACM CCS'02, 18–22 November 2002, pp. 41–47.

ETSI TR103 167 v0.3.1 , 2011. Machine to machine communications (M2M); threat analysis and counter-measures to M2M service layer.

Gont, F., Security assessment of the internet protocol version 6 (IPv6), UK Centre for the Protection of National Infrastructure.

Hamid, M.A., Rashid, M-O., Hong, C.S., 2006. Routing security in sensor network: Hello flood attack and defense IEEE ICNEWS, 2–4 January, Dhaka.

Hepp, M., Siorpaes, K., Bachlechner, D., 2007. Harvesting wiki consensus: Using wikipedia entries as vocabulary for knowledge management. Internet Computing, IEEE 11 (5), 54–65.

Hollar, S., 2000. COTS Dust, Master's Thesis, Electrical Engineering and Computer Science Department, UC Berkeley, 2000.

Hu, Y.-C., Perrig, A., Johnson, D.B., 2003. Packet leashes: a defense against wormhole attacks in wireless networks, Twenty-Second Annual Joint Conference of the IEEE Computer and Communications Societies. IEEE INFOCOM 2003, vol. 3, 30 March–3 April 2003, pp. 1976–1986.

Jolly, G., Kuscu, M.C., Kokate, P., Younis, M., 2003. A low-energy key management protocol for wireless sensor networks. Proceedings of the Eighth IEEE International Symposium on Computers and Communication (ISCC 2003). vol. 1, pp. 335–340.

Karakehayov, Z., 2005. Using REWARD to detect team black-hole attacks in wireless sensor networks. In: Workshop on Real-World Wireless Sensor Networks (REALWSN'05), 20–21 June, Stockholm, Sweden.

Karlof, C., Wagner, D., 2003. Secure routing in wireless sensor networks: attacks and countermeasures. Elsevier's Ad Hoc Network Journal, Special Issue on Sensor Network Applications and Protocols, September, pp. 293–315.

Karlof, C., Sastry, N., Wagner, D., 2004. TinySec: a link layer security architecture for wireless sensor networks. Proceedings of the 2nd International Conference on Embedded Networked Sensor Systems, Baltimore, MD, USA, pp. 162–175.

Kim, C.H., O, S.C., Lee, S., Yang, W.I., Lee, H-W., 2003. Steganalysis on BPCS Steganography. Pacific Rim Workshop on Digital Steganography (STEG'03), 3–4 July, Japan.

Kulkarni, S.S., Gouda, M.G., Arora, A., 2005. Secret instantiation in adhoc networks, Special Issue of Elsevier Journal of Computer Communications on Dependable Wireless Sensor Networks, May pp. 1–15.

Kurak, C., McHugh, J., 1992. A cautionary note on image downgrading in computer security applications. Proceedings of the 8th Computer Security Applications Conference, San Antonio, December, pp. 153–159.

Mokowitz, I.S., Longdon, G.E., Chang, L., 2001. A new paradigm hidden in steganography. Proceedings of the 2000 Workshop on New Security Paradigms, Ballycotton, County Cork, Ireland, pp. 41–50.

Newsome, J., Shi, E., Song, D, Perrig, A, 2004. The sybil attack in sensor networks: analysis & defenses. Proceedings of the Third International Symposium on Information Processing in Sensor Networks, ACM, pp. 259–268.

NIST selects winner of secure hash algorithm (SHA-3) competition, 2 October 2012. <http://www.nist.gov/itl/csd/sha-100212.cfm>.

Oniz, C.C, Tasci, S.E, Savas, E., Ercetin, O., Levi, A, SeFER: secure, flexible and efficient routing protocol for distributed sensor networks. <http://people.sabanciuniv.edu/ ∼ levi/SeFER_EWSN.pdf>.

Orihashi, M., Nakagawa, Y., Murakami, Y., Kobayashi, K., 2003. Channel synthesized modulation employing singular vector for secured access on physical layer. IEEE GLOBECOM, vol. 3, 1226–1230, 1–5 December 2003.

Pathan, A.-S.K., Alam, M., Monowar, M., Rabbi, F., 2004. An efficient routing protocol for mobile ad hoc networks with neighbor awareness and multicasting. Proceedings of the IEEE E-Tech, Karachi, 31 July, pp. 97−100.

Pathan, A-S.K., Islam, H.K., Sayeed, S.A., Ahmed, F. Hong, C.S., 2006. A framework for providing e-services to the rural areas using wireless ad hoc and sensor networks IEEE ICNEWS.

Perrig, A., Szewczyk, R., Wen, V., Culler, D., Tygar, J.D., 2002. SPINS: security protocols for sensor networks. Wireless Networks 8 (5), 521−534.

Pfleeger, C.P., Pfleeger, S.L., 2003. Security in Computing. Third ed. Prentice Hall, Upper Saddle River, NJ.

Rabaey, J.M., Ammer, J., Karalar, T., Suetfei Li., Otis, B., Sheets, M., Tuan, T., 2002. PicoRadios for wireless sensor networks: the next challenge in ultra-low power design. 2002 IEEE International Solid-State Circuits Conference (ISSCC 2002), vol. 1, 3−7 February, pp. 200−201.

Saleh, M., Khatib, I.A., 2005. Throughput analysis of WEP security in ad hoc sensor networks. Proceedings of the Second International Conference on Innovations in Information Technology (IIT'05), 26−28 September, Dubai.

Slijepcevic, S., Potkonjak, M., Tsiatsis, V., Zimbeck, S., Srivastava, M.B., 2002. On communication security in wireless ad-hoc sensor networks. 11th IEEE International Workshops on Enabling Technologies: Infrastructure for Collaborative Enterprises, 10−12 June 2002, pp. 139−144.

Steven Cherry with Ralph Langner, 2010. How Stuxnet is rewriting the cyberterrorism playbook. October IEEE Spectrum.

Strulo, B., Farr, J., Smith, A., 2003. Securing mobile ad hoc networks—a motivational approach. BT Technol. J. 21 (3), 81−89.

Undercoffer, J., Avancha, S., Joshi, A., Pinkston, J., 2002. Security for sensor networks. CADIP Research Symposium, available at <http://www.cs.sfu.ca/ ∼ angiez/personal/paper/sensor-ids.pdf>.

Valerie Aurora, 2012. Lifetimes of cryptographic hash functions, <http://valerieaurora.org/hash.html>.

Wang, B-T., Schulzrinne, H., 2004. An IP traceback mechanism for reflective DoS attacks. Canadian Conference on Electrical and Computer Engineering, vol. 2, 2−5 May, pp. 901−904.

Wood, A.D., Stankovic, J.A., 2002. Denial of service in sensor networks. Computer 35 (10), 54−62.

Wood, A.D., Stankovic, J.A., Son, S.H., 2003. JAM: a jammed-area mapping service for sensor networks. 24th IEEE Real-Time Systems Symposium, RTSS, pp. 286−297.

Yang, H., Luo, H., Ye, F., Lu, S., Zhang, L., 2004. Security in Mobile Ad Hoc Networks: Challenges and Solutions. IEEE Wireless Commun. 11 (1), 38−47, February.

Ye, F., Luo, H., Lu, S., Zhang, L., 2005. Statistical en-route filtering of injected false data in sensor networks. IEEE J. Select. Areas Commun. 23 (4), 839−850.

Younis, M., Youssef, M., Arisha, K., 2002. Energy-aware routing in cluster-based sensor networks. Proceeding of the 10th IEEE International Symposium on Modeling, Analysis and Simulation of Computer and Telecommunications Systems, 1−16 October, pp. 129−136.

Younis, M., Akkaya, K., Eltoweissy, M., Wadaa, A., 2004. On handling QoS traffic in wireless sensor networks. Proceedings of the 37th Annual Hawaii International Conference on System Sciences, 5−8 January, 2004, pp. 292−301.

Yuan, L., Qu, G., 2002. Design space exploration for energy-efficient secure sensor network. Proceedings of the IEEE International Conference on Application-Specific Systems, Architectures and Processors, 17−19 July 2002, pp. 88−97.

Zhou, L., Haas, Z.J., 1999. Securing ad hoc networks. IEEE. Networks 13 (6), 24−30.

CHAPTER 7

Existing Security Scheme for IoT

Imed Romdhani

We introduce the main Internet of things (IoT) security concepts while highlighting the differences between them. Then, we propose an in-depth discussion and critic of existing security approaches in the literature.

7.1 DATA SECURITY AND PRIVACY

Privacy and security are often used interchangeably. Although these two concepts are closely related, important differences exist. In fact, privacy is related to persons. It ensures that persons keep control over the information they disclose in the context of a particular application (e.g., on the Internet). Indeed, ensuring privacy means that personal information disclosed for a specific purpose with specific entities are not made available to other unauthorized entities, and not exploited to infer further information. Security on its side is related to data, and usually referred in the literature to the different means that are deployed in order to guarantee a set of properties. In the following, we provide a brief definition of each property.

- *Confidentiality*: ensures that, apart from the authorized involved entities, the exchanged data during a communication are kept confidential. Confidentiality is generally ensured through encryption.
- *Integrity and Authenticity*: integrity ensures that exchanged data between two entities during a communication process has not been altered by unauthorized entities. However, authenticity validates the origin of the data. Message Authentication Code (MAC) messages are used to provide both properties.
- *Availability* ensures that data are available when needed by authorized entities. This implies that the communication system has to remain functional despite security attacks (i.e., Denial of Service) and hardware failures. Backup systems and redundancy are used as a means to provide availability.

Securing the Internet of Things. DOI: http://dx.doi.org/10.1016/B978-0-12-804458-2.00007-X
© 2017 Elsevier Inc. All rights reserved.

- *Nonrepudiation*: ensures the means to verify that an entity has actually participated in an exchange of information, such as sending/receiving information or a digital signature.
- *Access control*: ensures that the involved entities are authorized to be part of the communication, and that protected information is only accessed by authorized entities. Access control is usually ensured through three successive steps. *Identification* which is a claim of identity (i.e., who someone is or what something is). This claim is then verified through *Authentication*. This step ensures that the identities provided by the involved entities are correct. Upon successful identification and authentication, *Authorization* allows to determine what information can be accessed and what actions can be carried out.

The relationship between security and privacy is that security is necessary but not sufficient to protect privacy. In fact, any breach in security properties, in particular data confidentiality, will have a direct impact on privacy. Nevertheless, even though security properties are ensured, voluntarily disclosed data can be used by malicious entities to infer information for illegal purposes.

7.2   DATA CONFIDENTIALITY AND KEY MANAGEMENT

Ensuring data confidentiality is crucial for IoT applications. In fact, any failure would seriously threaten users' privacy. Thus, a wide deployment of IoT applications might be hindered. To provide data confidentiality, cryptographic algorithms are generally employed to cipher data. Doing so, even if the exchanged data is eavesdropped, the attacker will not be able to access its content. In contrast to the *security by obscurity* principle, Kerckhoffs principle (Kerckhoffs, 1883) states that a cryptosystem should rely on the secrecy of the keys. In fact, this principle assumes that an attacker is able to access and master the cryptographic protocol. Its strength should then be placed in the secrecy of the keys. Cryptographic algorithms are categorized into two main categories.

- *Symmetric protocols*: in this category of algorithms, the same shared key between the involved entities is used to encrypt and decrypt data. The main drawback of symmetric encryption is the requirement that the involved parties have access to the shared secret key. In fact, establishing a secure channel to distribute the secret key is challenging. However, symmetric protocols are less resource consuming compared to asymmetric protocols (De Meulenaer et al., 2008). MAC messages are computed using symmetric algorithms. Their aim is to provide authenticity and integrity. In fact, MAC messages are computed using an input of a hash function (e.g., HMAC) the exchanged message and the shared symmetric key. The receiver computes its own MAC using the same shared key and compares it with the received one. If the two MAC messages are identical, it implies that the message has not being altered, thus, ensuring integrity. Otherwise, the two MAC messages would not have been identical. In addition, the compatibility of the two MAC messages also indicates that the message is authentic as it ensures that an entity in possession of the shared symmetric key has sent the message. Advanced Encryption Standard-Counter with Cipher Block Chaining-Message Authentication Code (AES-CCM) mode that defines Advanced Encryption Standard (AES) Cipher Algorithm in Cipher Block Chaining (CBC) Mode for MAC generation with AES Counter Mode (AES-CTR) for encryption are examples of symmetric protocols (Dworkin, 2007).

— *Asymmetric protocols*: in this category of algorithms, a pair of public/private keys is used in the encryption/decryption process. The encrypting entity uses the public key of the receiver to encrypt data. Public keys are not kept secret. To decrypt the encrypted message, the receiver uses its private key. Unlike public keys, private keys are kept secret and only available to their owner. Digital signatures are based on asymmetric protocols. In fact, an entity can sign a message by encrypting it using its private key. The receiving entity uses the public key of the sending entity to check the signature. Digital signatures provide authentication of the source of a message. Indeed, private keys are bound to a specific entity. Hence, a valid signature proves that a message is actually sent by that specific entity. Digital signatures also provide integrity considering that if a message is altered during its transmission, the signature would no longer be valid. Furthermore, nonrepudiation is also guaranteed as the access to the signing private key is limited to its owner. The main drawback of asymmetric protocols in the context of IoT is their high energy cost compared to symmetric protocols (De Meulenaer et al., 2008). Rivest-Shamir-Adleman (RSA) and elliptic curve cryptography are examples of asymmetric cryptographic primitives (Gura et al., 2004).

Kerckhoffs principle is widely adopted in the design of security systems (Shannon, 1949). Thus, key management protocols represent the cornerstone of any cryptographic system. They are in charge of generating and distributing the required keying materials. Key management protocols can be gathered into two main categories of approaches (Roman et al., 2011a).

— *Preshared approaches*: These are based on the presharing of keying materials between the two entities willing to secure their communications. These keying materials are used to derive a secret shared key. The major issue with these approaches is the initial distribution of the keying materials. In fact, the distribution is prior to any exchange of information. As a result, these protocols are not applicable between two entities that have not established upstream a shared context. Nevertheless, preshared approaches offer a negligible computation overhead as no complex operation is required to establish the shared secret.

- *Public key approaches*: These are based on asymmetric primitives to establish a shared secret between two entities that have no previous preestablished context. The main issue with public key approaches is their high computation overhead. For instance, Diffie-Hellman key exchange protocol (Rescorla, 1999) uses exponential operations that are costly in particular for the constrained entities of the IoT (Wander et al., 2005). However, public key approaches offer the ability of establishing a secret between previously unknown entities, which might be necessary for future dynamic IoT applications.

To assess key management protocols, several properties are taken into consideration (Shirey, 2000, 2007).

- *Distribution*: This property is considered regarding the process through which the initial information used in the key establishment is distributed. This distribution can be achieved in an offline mode or in an online mode. In the offline mode, the required information is set upstream. On the other side, the online mode allows the involved entities to engage in an exchange process without any preestablished context. In the context of the dynamic IoT, the protocols that allow an online mode distribution are preferred.
- *Authentication*: This property ensures that the entities involved in the key exchange are authenticated. This can either be achieved through the use of digital signatures in the case of public key approaches, or through the initial shared secret in the case of preshared approaches. Authentication is highly sought in IoT applications as the authenticity of data sources is crucial, in particular, for sensitive applications.
- *Extensibility*: This property is related to the possibility of involving further entities after the initial key exchange. In fact, in some key management protocols, the number of entities that can be involved in the key exchange process is limited. Extensibility is an essential property for IoT applications where the number of connected objects is high.
- *Resilience*: A key management protocol is resilient if the corruption of one entity, and thus the extraction of secret information, has limited consequences on the overall system. Ensuring this property for IoT applications would definitely strengthen the security level. In fact, entities in the context of IoT will likely remain unattended for long

period of time, which make them vulnerable to physical attacks and corruption.
- *Scalability*: This property is ensured if the number of cryptographic materials stored in an entity does not scale linearly (or worst exponentially) with the implication of new entities in the key exchange process. Scalability is highly sought for IoT applications as the number of connected objects is expected to grow significantly.
- *Collusion freedom*: This property is related to the fact that any set of corrupted users are unable to access the generated secret.

Group communications (multicast) constitute an important component of future IoT communication. They include one-to-many, many-to-many, and many-to-one communications. To secure these types of communications, group key management protocols (GKMPs) are used. These latter are in charge of generating, distributing, and maintaining a shared secret key. In addition to the required security properties of two parties' key management protocols, two main security properties have to be ensured in GKMPs (Challal and Seba, 2005).

- *Backward secrecy*: This property is related to the dynamic of group members. When a new member joins a group, exchanged information before its arrival can be accessed. In fact, if the new member has previously stored the exchanged information, it would be possible to decrypt them after the receipt of the group key. Backward secrecy ensures that a new member cannot access communications that have taken place before its joining.
- *Forward secrecy*: This property is considered in the case of a member departure. Forward secrecy is provided when a leaving member is not able to decrypt exchanged information after it leaves the group.

7.3 LITERATURE REVIEW

There is a huge literature on how security issues could hinder IoT deployment. In fact, studies have shown that security in any IoT application will be crucial as billions of intelligent things will cooperate with each other in a random and unpredictable way (Roman et al., 2011b; Medaglia and Serbanati, 2010; Miorandi et al., 2012; Weber, 2010).

The creation of a secure channel between gateways and objects (i.e., nodes) is crucial to implement security mechanisms. To establish this channel, key management protocols are required to allow two remote devices to negotiate security credentials. Various approaches have been proposed in the literature to deal with the key establishment process. For instance, Public Key Cryptography could be suitable if used only in early stages of a key establishment process (Malan et al., 2004). Moreover, the preshared keys solutions could be used in limited real-life scenarios where the distribution of keys in an offline mode is possible (Prashar and Vashisht, 2012). Besides, key pool paradigm includes several approaches that improve scalability while sacrificing their key connectivity (Eschenauer and Gligor, 2002).

Several approaches aim to tailor security protocols for the IP-based IoT. The main focus of these works is to make standard-based security protocols suitable for constrained IoT environments. In particular, several compression schemes for the IP-based IoT have been proposed. The compression of IPv6 headers, extension headers along with UDP (User Datagram Protocol) headers has been standardized through the 6LoWPAN adaptation layer in Montenegro et al. (2007) and Hui and Thubert (2011). Moreover, authors in Granjal et al. (2010) and Raza et al. (2011) have presented 6LoWPAN-based compression techniques for IPsec payload headers: AH (Authentication Header) and ESP (Encapsulating Security Payload) have been later standardized in Raza et al. (2013). Besides, an IKE (Internet Key Exchange) compression scheme has been also proposed in order to provide a lightweight automatic way to establish security associations for IPsec (Raza et al., 2012b). Likewise, header compression layers for DTLS (Datagram Transport Layer Security), HIP DEX (Host Identity Protocol Diet Exchange), and HIP BEX (HIP Base Exchange) were respectively introduced in Raza et al. (2012a), Hummen et al. (2013a), and Sahraoui and Bilami (2015).

Apart from packet compression schemes, further design improvement approaches have been introduced to tailor security protocols to the IoT. Authors, in Hummen et al. (2013b), have proposed complementary lightweight extensions to HIP DEX that could be generalized to DTLS and IKE. Following the same way, authors in Hummen et al. (2013c) have introduced design ideas to reduce the overhead of the DTLS handshake where their primary goal was to make the use of certificates for authentication purposes viable in IoT contexts. Moreover, to offload the computational load to third parties, delegation procedures of protocol primitives have been proposed. Authors in Saied and Olivereau (2012a, 2012b, 2012c) have introduced collaboration for HIP. Their idea is to take advantage of more powerful nodes in the neighborhood of a constrained node to carry heavy computations in a distributed way. Likewise, IKE session establishment delegation to a gateway has been proposed in Bonetto et al. (2012). Furthermore, authors in Freeman et al. (2007) have introduced a delegation procedure that enables a client to delegate certificate validation to a trusted server. While the proposed delegation approaches reduce the computational load at the constrained nodes, they break the end-to-end principle by requiring a trusted third party.

GKMPs have traditionally been classified in the literature into three main categories: centralized, distributed, and decentralized (Daghighi et al., 2015; Rafaeli and Hutchison, 2003; Romdhani et al., 2004).

Several approaches have been proposed within the centralized category. In this category, the key management is ensured by a central entity called Key Management Server (KMS). The KMS is a powerful entity that is in charge of rekeying the entire group. To do so, a trusted channel is established between the KMS and the nodes of the group during an initialization phase. This channel is then used to securely rekey the group. Authors in Harney and Muckenhirn (1997) have proposed the GKMP. In this protocol, the KMS maintains a Group Key Packet (GKP) that contains a Group Traffic Encryption Key (GTEK) to secure the traffic, and a Group Key Encryption Key (GKEK) to secure the transmission of the GKP. Upon a join event, the KMS uses the old GTEK to distribute the new GKP. However, upon a leave event, the KMS sends the new GKP as a unicast message to each member. This engenders a $O(n)$ complexity, which makes this protocol not scalable to large and dynamic networks. Authors in Veltri et al. (2013) have introduced an interval-based centralized protocol. The proposed protocol predicts when members might leave the group. In fact, when a member first joins the group, the KMS transmits the required keying materials for the period of time during which the member intends to be part of the group. When the period expires, the member can leave the group without triggering a rekeying event. However, this approach brings several drawbacks. Indeed, predicting the leaving time of members is not realistic and practical for highly dynamic networks. Furthermore, constrained members planning to remain for a long period of time in the group risk to suffer from storage issues. Hence, this protocol is not tailored to dynamic networks with high number of unpredictable leaving events such as the IoT context.

The Secure Lock protocol introduced in Chiou and Chen (1989) is based on the Chinese Remainder theorem. The basic idea is to rekey the group with a single broadcast instead of peer-to-peer messages. This approach minimizes the number of exchanged messages at the expense of a high computational cost. This cost is due to the Chinese Remainder calculation before each rekeying. Hierarchical-based protocols, such as the Logical Key Hierarchy (LKH) protocol (Wong et al., 2000) and the One-way Function Tree protocol that improves LKH (Balenson et al., 1999), intend to further reduce the rekeying cost (i.e., $O\text{Log}(n)$). These protocols are based on a KMS, which shares Key Encryption Keys (KEK) with subgroups of the network. Upon a rekeying event, the KMS uses the shared secret with the subgroups that are unknown to the concerned members to distribute the new TEK. Thus, the number of required rekeying messages is reduced. In brief, centralized protocols take advantage of symmetric algorithms, and avoid peer-to-peer communications within the group. Nevertheless, they still suffer from the single point of failure and the scalability issue.

In distributed protocols, the members collaborate in the rekeying process, and therefore there is no need for a central entity as in centralized protocols.

However, peer-to-peer communications are still required between members. Tree-based Group Diffie-Hellman protocol (TGDH) (Kim et al., 2004), which was later improved by Lee et al. (2006) is based on a hierarchical binary tree. Each node of the tree is associated with two types of keys: a secret key and a blinded one (public). TGDH relies on the classical two-party Diffie-Hellman protocol. Hence, the calculation of a nonleaf node secret key is based on the knowledge of the secret key of one child and the blinded key of the other one. In one word, distributed protocols offer the advantage of being highly reliable as they do not rely on a single trusted entity. Nevertheless, full peer-to-peer communications between the group members are required. In addition, distributed protocols generate a large amount of exchanged messages in addition to the use of complex asymmetric operations.

Decentralized protocols divide the network into several areas. Each area is associated with a hierarchical level. A KMS is in charge of ensuring the key management process for each area. Traditionally, this category is further classified into two subcategories (Daghighi et al., 2015): the common TEK per area (Briscoe, 1999; Rafaeli and Hutchison, 2002), and the independent TEK per area (Piao et al., 2013; Mehdizadeh et al., 2014). In the first subcategory, the same TEK is used to secure communications across the different areas of the group. This avoids data translations between the areas. However, when a rekeying event occurs, all group members are affected. Hence, this category is affected by the *1-affects-n* issue. The second category mitigates this issue as each rekeying concerns only the area where a new key needs to be established. As a result, data path is affected. In fact, data passing from an area to another has to be translated at the edge of each area. In Challal and Seba (2005), the authors classify the decentralized protocols into Time-Driven rekeying subcategory (Briscoe, 1999; Setia et al., 2000) and Membership-Driven rekeying subcategory (Rafaeli and Hutchison, 2002; Ballardie, 1996). In the Time-Driven approach, a rekeying is triggered after the end of each interval of time regardless of membership events. This approach reduces the number of exchanged messages by triggering one rekeying for several events. Nevertheless, a leaving member would be able to communicate until the end of the interval. Similarly, a new joining member would have to wait the beginning of a new interval before being able to access data. In the Membership-Driven subcategory, the group key is changed upon each membership event.

The pervasiveness and distributivity of IoT applications make mobility as one of the most important IoT specificities. However, most of the above-cited approaches do not take into consideration members' mobility from an area to another. Instead, mobility is considered as a leave from the source area, and a joining to the destination area. This vision implies a rekeying for both areas. IoT resources scarcity makes this solution not feasible. In fact, few works have been proposed in the literature to efficiently handle mobility in GKMPs (Gharout et al., 2012; Kamat et al., 2003). Indeed, to reduce the rekeying overhead, these solutions consider that forward secrecy is inherently achieved. Doing so, the number of exchanged messages is reduced by avoiding a rekeying operation in the source area at the expense of forward secrecy violation. In addition, a list that handles the mobile members is generally implemented in the KMSs. In large and highly dynamic networks such as IoT, maintaining a list of moving members might quickly become highly complex to manage.

References

Balenson, D., McGrew, D., Sherman, A., February 1999. Key management for large dynamic groups: one-way function trees and amortized initialization. Internet-Draft.

Ballardie, A., May 1996. Scalable multicast key distribution. RFC 1949.

Bonetto, R., Bui, N., Lakkundi, V., Olivereau, A., Serbanati, A., Rossi, M., 2012. Secure communication for smart iot objects: protocol stacks, use cases and practical examples. In: International Symposium on a World of Wireless, Mobile and Multimedia Networks (WoWMoM). IEEE, pp. 1–7.

Briscoe, B., 1999. Marks: zero side effect multicast key management using arbitrarily revealed key sequences. In: Networked Group Communication, pp. 301–320.

Challal, Y., Seba, H., 2005. Group key management protocols: a novel taxonomy. Int. J. Inf. Technol. 2 (1), 105–118.

Chiou, G.H., Chen, W.T., 1989. Secure broadcasting using the secure lock. IEEE Trans. Software Eng. 15 (8), 929–934.

Daghighi, B., Kiah, M.L.M., Shamshirband, S., Rehman, M.H.U., 2015. Toward secure group communication in wireless mobile environments: issues, solutions, and challenges. J. Network Comput. Appl. 50, 1–14.

De Meulenaer, G., Gosset, F., Standaert, F.X., Pereira, O., 2008. On the energy cost of communication and cryptography in wireless sensor networks. In: IEEE International Conference on Wireless and Mobile Computing, Networking and Communication, pp. 580–585.

Dworkin, M., 2007. Recommendation for block cipher modes of operation: the CCM. Mode for authentication and confidentiality. SP-800-38c, NIST, US Department of Commerce.

Eschenauer, L., Gligor, V.D., 2002. A key management scheme for distributed sensor networks. In: Ninth ACM Conference on Computer and Communications Security, pp. 41–47.

Freeman, T., Housley, R., Malpani, A., Cooper, D., Polk, W., 2007. Server-based certicate validation protocol (scvp). Internet Proposed Standard RFC 5055.

Gharout, S., Bouabdallah, A., Challal, Y., Achemlal, M., 2012. Adaptive group key management protocol for wireless communications. J. Univers. Comput. Sci. 18 (6), 874–898.

Granjal, J., Monteiro, E., Sa Silva, J., 2010. Enabling network-layer security on ipv6 wireless sensor networks. In: Proceedings of IEEE GLOBECOM.

Gura, N., Patel, A., Wander, A., Elberle, H., Shantz, S.C., 2004. Comparing elliptic curve cryptography and rsa on 8-bit cpus. In: Proceedings of the Sixth Workshop on Cryptographic Hardware and Embedded Systems (CHES 2004), pp. 119–132.

Harney, H., Muckenhirn, C., July 1997. Group key management protocol (gkmp) architecture. Internet Engineering Task Force, RFC 2093.

Hui, J., Thubert, P., 2011. Compression format for ipv6 datagrams over IEEE 802.15.4-based networks. Internet Engineering Task Force, RFC 6282.

Hummen, R., Hiller, J., Henze, M., Wehrle, K., 2013a. Slimfit—a HIP dex compression layer for the ip-based internet of things. In: WiMob, IEEE, pp. 259–266.

Hummen, R., Wirtz, H., Ziegeldorf, J.H., Hiller, J., Wehrle, K., 2013b. Tailoring end-to-end ip security protocols to the internet of things. In: 21st International Conference on Network Protocols (ICNP). IEEE, pp. 1–10.

Hummen, R., Ziegeldorf, J.H., Shafagh, H., Raza, S., Wehrle, K., 2013c. Towards viable certicate-based authentication for the internet of things. In: HotWiSec'13 Proceedings of the Second ACM Workshop on Hot Topics on Wireless Network Security and Privacy, pp. 37–42.

Kamat, S., Parimi, S., Agrawal, D.P., 2003. Reduction in control overhead for a secure, scalable framework for mobile multicast. IEEE Int. Conf. Commun., ICC'03 1, 98–103.

Kerckhoffs, A., 1883. La cryptographie militaire. J. Sci. Mil. XI, 161–191.

Kim, Y., Perrig, A., Tsudik, G., 2004. Tree-based group key agreement. ACM Trans. Inf. Syst. Secur. 7 (1), 60–96.

Lee, P., Lui, J., Yau, D., 2006. Distributed collaborative key agreement and authentication protocols for dynamic peer groups. IEEE/ACM Trans. Networking 14 (2), 263–276.

Malan, D., Welsh, M., Smith, M., 2004. A public-key infrastructure for key distribution in tiny os based on elliptic curve cryptography. In: First Annual IEEE Communications Society Conference on Sensor and Ad Hoc Communications and Networks, pp. 71–80.

Medaglia, C.M., Serbanati, A., 2010. An overview of privacy and security issues in the internet of things. In: The Internet of Things, pp. 389–395.

Mehdizadeh, A., Hashim, F., Othman, M., 2014. Lightweight decentralized multicast-unicast key management method in wireless ipv6 networks. J. Network Comput. Appl. 42, 59–69.

Miorandi, D., Sicari, S., De Pellegrini, F., Chlamtac, I., 2012. Internet of things: vision, applications and research challenges. Ad Hoc Networks 10 (7), 1497–1516.

Montenegro, G., Kushalnagar, N., Hui, J., Culler, D., 2007. Transmission of ipv6 packets over IEEE 802.15.4 networks. Internet Engineering Task Force, RFC 4944.

Piao, Y., Kim, J., Tariq, U., Hong, M., 2013. Polynomial-based key management for secure intra-group and inter-group communication. Comput. Math. Appl. 65 (9), 1300–1309.

Prashar, M., Vashisht, R., 2012. Survey on pre-shared keys in wireless sensor network. Int. J. Sci. Emerging Technol. Latest Trends 4 (1), 42–48.

Rafaeli, S., Hutchison, D., June 2002. Hydra: a decentralized group key management. In: 11th IEEE International WETICE: Enterprise Security Workshop.

Rafaeli, S., Hutchison, D., 2003. A survey of key management for secure group communication. ACM Comput. Surv. 35 (3), 309–329.

Raza, S., Duquennoy, S., Chung, T., Yazar, D., Voigt, T., Roedig, U., 2011. Securing communication in 6lowpan with compressed ipsec. In: Proceedings of IEEE DCOSS.

Raza, S., Trabalza, D., Voigt, T., 2012a. 6lowpan compressed dtls for coap. In: Proceedings of IEEE DCOSS.

Raza, S., Voigt, T., Jutvik, V., 2012b. Lightweight ikev2: a key management solution for both compressed ipsec and IEEE 802.15.4 security. In: IETF/IAB Workshop on Smart Object Security.

Raza, S., Duquennoy, S., Selander, G., 2013. Compression of IPsec AH and ESP headers for constrained environments. Draft-raza-6lowpanipsec-00 (WiP), IETF.

Rescorla, E., 1999. Diffie−Hellman key agreement method. Internet Engineering Task Force, RFC 2631.

Roman, R., Alcaraz, C., Lopez, J., Sklavos, N., 2011a. Key management systems for sensor networks in the context of internet of things. Comput. Electr. Eng. 37 (2), 147−159.

Roman, R., Najera, P., Lopez, J., 2011b. Securing the internet of things. IEEE Comput. 44, 51−58.

Romdhani, I., Kellil, M., Hong-Yon, L., Bouabdallah, A., Bettahar, H., 2004. IP mobile multicast: challenges and solutions. IEEE Commun. Surv. Tutorials 6, 18−41.

Sahraoui, S., Bilami, A., 2015. Efficient HIP-based approach to ensure lightweight end-to-end security in the internet of things. Comput. Networks 91, 26−45.

Saied, Y.B., Olivereau, A., 2012a. D-hip: a distributed key exchange scheme for hip-based internet of things. In: Proceedings of IEEE WoWMoM.

Saied, Y.B., Olivreau, A., October 24−25, 2012b. (k, n) Threshold distributed key exchange for HIP based internet of things. In: Proceedings of the 10th ACM International Symposium on Mobility Management and Wireless Access, pp. 79−86.

Saied, Y.B., Olivereau, A., 2012c. Hip tiny exchange (tex): a distributed key exchange scheme for hip-based internet of things. In: Proceedings of ComNet.

Setia, S., Koussih, S., Jajodia, S., Harder, E., 2000. Kronos: a scalable group re-keying approach for secure multicast. In: Proceedings IEEE Symposium on Security and Privacy, pp. 215−228.

Shannon, C.E., 1949. Communication theory of secrecy systems. Bell Syst. Tech. J. 28 (4), 656−715.

Shirey, R., 2000. RFC 2828: internet security glossary. The Internet Society, p. 13.

Shirey, R., 2007. Internet security glossary, version 2. Internet Engineering Task Force, RFC 4949.

Veltri, L., Cirani, S., Busanelli, S., Ferrari, G., 2013. A novel batch-based group key management protocol applied to the internet of things. Ad Hoc Networks 11 (8), 2724−2737.

Wander, A., Gura, N., Eberle, H., Gupta, V., Shantz, S.C., 2005. Energy analysis of public-key cryptography for wireless sensor networks. In: Third IEEE International Conference on Pervasive Computing and Communications. PerCom 2005, pp. 324−328.

Weber, R.H., 2010. Internet of things, new security and privacy challenges. Comput. Law Secur. Rev. 26 (1), 23−30.

Wong, C.K., Gouda, M., Lam, S.S., 2000. Secure group communications using key graphs. IEEE/ACM Trans. Networking 8 (1), 16−30.

Further Reading

Ameen, M.A., Liu, J., Kwak, K., 2012. Security and privacy issues in wireless sensor networks for healthcare applications. J. Med. Syst. 36, 93−101.

Atzori, L., Iera, A., Morabito, G., 2010. The internet of things: a survey. Comput. Networks 54, 2787−2805.

Atzori, L., Iera, A., Morabito, G., Nitti, M., 2012. The social internet of things (siot) when social networks meet the internet of things: concept, architecture and network characterization. Comput. Networks 56 (16), 3594−3608.

Atzori, L., Iera, A., Morabito, G., 2014. From "smart objects" to "social objects": the next evolutionary step of the internet of things. IEEE Commun. Mag. 52 (1), 97−105.

Dohr, A., Modre-Opsrian, R., Drobics, M., Hayn, D., Schreier, G., April 2010. The internet of things for ambient assisted living. In: Information Technology: New Generations (ITNG), pp. 804−809.

Istepanian, R., Jara, A., Sungoor, A., Philips, N., 2010. Internet of things for m-health applications (iomt). In: AMA-IEEE Medical Technology Conference on Individualized Healthcare, Washington, DC.

Javadi, S.S., Razzaque, M.A., 2013. Security and privacy in wireless body area networks for health care applications. In: Wireless Networks and Security, pp. 165−187.

Karlof, C., Wagner, D., 2003. Secure routing in wireless sensor networks: attacks and countermeasures. Ad Hoc Networks 1 (2), 293−315.

Li, M., Lou, W., February 2010. Data security and privacy in wireless body area networks. In: Wireless Technologies for E-Healthcare.

Lim, S., Oh, T.H., Choi, Y.B., Lakshman, T., February 2010. Security issues on wireless body area network for remote healthcare monitoring. In: Sensor Networks, Ubiquitous, and Trustworthy Computing (SUTC), IEEE International Conference, pp. 327−332.

Ng, H.S., Sim, M.L., Tan, C.M., 2006. Security issues of wireless sensor networks in healthcare applications. BT Technol. J. 24 (2), 138−144.

Ortiz, A.M., Hussein, D., Park, S., Han, S.N., Crespi, N., 2014. The cluster between internet of things and social networks: review and research challenges. IEEE Int. Things J. 1 (3), 206−215.

Patel, M., Wang, J., 2010. Applications, challenges, and prospective in emerging body area networking technologies. IEEE Wireless Commun. 17 (1), 80−88.

Tsiftes, N., Dunkels, A., 2011. A database in every sensor. In: Proceedings of the Ninth ACM Conference on Embedded Networked Sensor Systems, pp. 316−332.

CHAPTER 8

Security Concerns in Social IoT

Imed Romdhani

Social Internet of Things (SIoT) (Atzori et al., 2012) establishes a link between social networks and IoT. The main idea is that a large number of individuals tied in a social network can provide far more accurate answers to complex problems than a single individual (even knowledgeable one). In the future, things will be associated to the services they can deliver. Thus, to better implement services within a given social network of objects, a key objective will be to publish information/services, find them, and discover novel resources. This can be achieved by navigating a social network of "friend" objects instead of relying on typical Internet discovery tools that cannot scale to the trillions of future devices.

Authors in Atzori et al. (2012) and Ortiz et al. (2014) affirm that social relationships among humans might be applicable to certain kinds of behaviors of typical objects implementing pervasive applications. There is no doubt that many applications and services should be associated with groups of objects, which will cooperate in order to reach the overall interest of providing services to users (e.g., the same idea is behind the approaches involving the use of swarm intelligence and swarm robotics).

SIoT relies upon basic kinds of relationships such as the *parental object relationship* (POR), which is established among objects belonging to the same production batch, or the *ownership object relationship* (OOR), which is based on heterogeneous objects belonging to the same user (e.g., mobile phones, game consoles, etc.). The establishment and the management of such relationships should occur without human intervention. Humans are only responsible for setting the rules of the objects and their social interactions. In a nutshell, SIoT makes the parallel between the current social networks and a future network of objects. The goal is to publish, find information, and discover novel resources to better implement the services. Nevertheless, SIoT

Securing the Internet of Things. DOI: http://dx.doi.org/10.1016/B978-0-12-804458-2.00008-1
© 2017 Elsevier Inc. All rights reserved.

may suffer (Atzori et al., 2014) from additional security threats compared to the classical IoT (not enhanced with social features). To bring SIoT to reality, objects have to be enhanced with cognitive capabilities. This will allow the objects to be more autonomous by taking initiatives such as sharing information, or connecting with another object. As a result, SIoT has to enforce additional security mechanisms to handle the additional features compared to the classical IoT. In fact, context-aware access control systems need to be developed while taking into consideration the complexity of the embedded cognitive capabilities. Furthermore, the design of security protocols has to be more energy aware in order to cope with the increased energy demand of the additional features.

References

Atzori, L., Iera, A., Morabito, G., Nitti, M., 2012. The social internet of things (SIoT) when social networks meet the internet of things: concept, architecture and network characterization. Comput. Networks 56 (16), 3594–3608.

Atzori, L., Iera, A., Morabito, G., 2014. From "smart objects" to "social objects": the next evolutionary step of the Internet of Things. IEEE Commun. Mag. 52 (1), 97–105.

Ortiz, A.M., Hussein, D., Park, S., Han, S.N., Crespi, N., 2014. The cluster between internet of things and social networks: review and research challenges. IEEE Internet Things J. 1 (3), 206–215.

CHAPTER 9

Confidentiality and Security for IoT Based Healthcare

Imed Romdhani

Internet of Things (IoT) deployment will open doors to a huge number of applications that would deeply improve our daily life. E-health applications are one of the typical applications that are gaining more and more attention (Atzori et al., 2010). An e-health system is defined as a radio-frequency-based wireless networking technology that provides ubiquitous networking functionalities. It is based on the interconnection of tiny nodes enhanced with sensing and/or actuating capabilities planted, or placed around the human body. E-health applications are context-aware, personal, dynamic, and anticipative by nature. As IoT is designed to meet these key characteristics, it provides a natural and suitable environment for their efficient deployment. In fact, an extensive research study on using IoT paradigm in e-health has been reported (Istepanian et al., 2010). Population aging and the increase of survival chances from disabling accidents and illnesses will lead to an increased demand from today's population that requires a continuous healthcare and monitoring (Dohr et al., 2010).

E-health applications could spare a patient from being admitted in hospitals for a long period of time. Reducing the number of nights that a patient may spend in a hospital and the associated risks that may result is a key area of focus for the medical community. Additionally, a continuous monitoring capability, if available, can anticipate the need for an emergency intervention. Moreover, early stage diagnostics could also be achieved remotely (Patel and Wang, 2010). In brief, e-health applications in the context of IoT constitute a cost-effective and unobtrusive solution that is of best interest of today's patients.

Nevertheless, as an IoT application (Atzori et al., 2010), e-health inherits the main IoT security threats and challenges. There is a huge literature on how security issues could hinder IoT deployment. In fact, studies have shown that security in any IoT application will be crucial as billions of intelligent things will cooperate with each other in a random and unpredictable way

133

Securing the Internet of Things. DOI: http://dx.doi.org/10.1016/B978-0-12-804458-2.00009-3
© 2017 Elsevier Inc. All rights reserved.

(Roman et al., 2011a; Medaglia and Serbanati, 2010; Miorandi et al., 2012; Weber, 2010). It has also been shown that even though IoT infrastructure is expected to involve protocols and interfaces similar to those running on Internet, it will be daunting to directly handle IoT threats based on classical known countermeasures due to the following:

- The scarcity of both power and computational resources will hinder classical solutions deployment.
- Distributivity and heterogeneity of the devices that will compose IoT (constrained and nonconstrained) might lead to gaps in end-to-end security.
- IoT will be highly scalable and dynamic, thus, traditional public key infrastructures need to be adapted to meet these requirements.
- Things will have to manage dynamic identities to deal with context-aware applications.
- Wireless connectivity will constitute the main media of communication, which could lead to different attacks such as eavesdropping and side channel attacks.
- Objects in IoT might be unattended for long period and thus are more vulnerable to physical attacks.

Moreover, studies by various authors (Li and Lou, 2010; Javadi and Razzaque, 2013; Lim et al., 2010; Ng et al., 2006) have underlined that e-health applications might be more vulnerable to attacks compared to other IoT applications as the generated data is highly sensitive and private. The health-related records are always private in nature, and any security breach in the confidentiality of such data would seriously repulse patients from adopting e-health solutions. For instance, many people would not like their personal health information, such as early stage of pregnancy or details of certain medical conditions, be divulged to third parties (Al Ameen et al., 2012). In fact, the eavesdropped communications could be used for several illegal purposes. Moreover, any eventual modification of health-related captured data could lead to disastrous consequences as it could engender wrong medical prescription or delay an emergency intervention.

Several attacks can threaten the establishment of secure channels (Li and Lou, 2010; Lim et al., 2010). In the following, we focus on the attacks that are positioned in the network and transport layer of the Open System Interconnection model.

Ensuring key freshness is an important security concern. Indeed, the involved entities have to be able to detect replayed messages. In particular, e-health applications might be more vulnerable facing this kind of attacks compared to other application scenarios; an outdated information could lead to inadequate medical interventions. To overcome this issue, nonces can be introduced in the different exchanged messages. In fact, these nonces could be implemented using one of the following strategies:

- Random numbers
- Sequence numbers
- Timestamps

Random numbers might constitute a solution for e-health scenarios. A smart object can maintain a list of the previous received random values in its internal memory. Upon receiving a new message, it checks if the nonce has already been received. As a result, replayed messages are detected. This solution brings a drawback; the smart object has to maintain a list of the received nonces in its internal memory. Nevertheless, due to recent advances in flash memory technology (Tsiftes and Dunkels, 2011), smart objects now provide a considerable amount of storage space, which attenuates the storage issue. The second solution is based on sequence numbers, which do not require any data storage. Indeed, sequence numbers provide a sequential counter in the exchanged messages. In case where a message is replayed, its counter will be smaller or equal to the current one. Thus, the message will be dropped. However, if one of the involved entities goes down (e.g., reboot, hardware failure, etc.), this protection is no longer effective. In fact, the involved entity will lose track of the current counter value. Besides, to ensure message freshness, timestamps could also be used. This solution is highly energy consuming to be implemented for constrained entities, as synchronized clocks have to be maintained. In a nutshell, protecting e-health applications against replayed messages could be achieved through the combination of the above-discussed strategies according to the network model specificities.

Denial of Service (DoS) attacks could seriously threaten the availability of e-health application. In fact, the gathered health-related data should always be available even if the system is under a DoS attack. Indeed, if any of the involved entities is made unavailable, in the sense that it is no longer able to gather or process data, this situation would engender disastrous consequences. To illustrate this aspect, let us assume that a smart object is planted in the body of a patient suffering from a heart condition. In case where a heart-related value that indicates an impending heart attack is registered, it should immediately be transmitted to healthcare services. Any delay due to a DoS attack could be fatal. Several mechanisms can be implemented to mitigate DoS attacks. Each exchanged message has to be authenticated upstream of any processing effort. In fact, no internal state is established before authenticating the different entities involved in an exchange. Besides, classical countermeasures could also be implemented such as rate-limiting and access control list. In addition, based on the sensitivity of e-health applications, redundancy can also be used. Whenever a smart object is made unavailable by a DoS attack, data exchanges carry on with the redundant node.

Sybil attacks, where a node claims multiple fake identities, could be highly harmful in the context of an e-health application. Through these attacks, an intruder could use feigned identities to send false information. As a result, either an actual emergency situation is skipped or ceaseless false emergency situations are thrown. Sybil attacks can be mitigated using different strategies based on the network model. Indeed, including the identity of the sender in the exchanged messages while ensuring authentication using a shared knowledge (i.e., key) is an efficient mechanism against Sybil attacks. Doing so, an attacker would not be able to use multiple identities authenticated with the same shared key. Furthermore, Sybil attacks can also be mitigated through the use of trusted certification to make sure that each entity is assigned exactly one identity.

Another point of interest with respect to the threat model of e-health applications is the attacks that aim to exhaust sensors energy making them unavailable. For instance, the desynchronization attack targets the sequence number of the exchanged messages. This will lead to infinite retransmissions, which waste both energy and bandwidth. Providing message integrity is the main security property that hinders this type of attacks. In fact, message authentication code messages can be computed and checked for each exchanged message ensuring that the included data has not been altered.

E-health applications are subject to several other attacks. In particular, routing attacks that can quickly hinder their functioning to the point of making them unavailable (Karlof and Wagner, 2003). Securing the routing process usually involves the introduction of intrusion detection systems (Karlof and Wagner, 2003).

References

Al Ameen, M., Liu, J., Kwak, K., 2012. Security and privacy issues in wireless sensor networks for healthcare applications. J Med Syst 36, 93–101.

Atzori, L., Iera, A., Morabito, G., 2010. The internet of things: a survey. Comput. Networks 54, 2787–2805.

Dohr, A., Modre-Opsrian, R., Drobics, M., Hayn, D., Schreier, G., April 2010. The internet of things for ambient assisted living. In Information Technology: New Generations (ITNG), pp. 804–809.

Istepanian, R., Jara, A., Sungoor, A., Philips, N., 2010. Internet of things for m-health applications (IOMT). AMA-IEEE medical technology conference on individualized healthcare, Washington, DC.

Javadi, S.S., Razzaque, M.A., 2013. Security and privacy in wireless body area networks for health care applications. Wireless Networks and Security 165–187.

Karlof, C., Wagner, D., 2003. Secure routing in wireless sensor networks: Attacks and counter-measures. Ad hoc Networks 1 (2), 293–315.

Li, M., Lou, W., 2010. Data security and privacy in wireless body area networks. Wireless Technol. E-healthcare.

Lim, S., Oh, T.H., Choi, Y.B., Lakshman, T., February 2010. Security issues on wireless body area network for remote healthcare monitoring. Sensor Networks, Ubiquitous, and Trustworthy Computing (SUTC), IEEE International Conference, pp. 327–332.

Medaglia, C.M., Serbanati, A., 2010. An overview of privacy and security issues in the internet of things. The internet of things, pp. 389–395.

Miorandi, D., Sicari, S., De Pellegrini, F., Chlamtac, I., 2012. Internet of things: vision, applications and research challenges. Ad Hoc Networks 1497–1516.

Ng, H.S., Sim, M.L., Tan, C.M., 2006. Security issues of wireless sensor networks in healthcare applications. Bri. Technol. J. 24 (2), 138–144.

Patel, M., Wang, J., 2010. Applications, challenges, and prospective in emerging body area networking technologies. Wireless Commun. 17, 80–88.

Roman, R., Najera, P., Lopez, J., 2011a. Securing the internet of things. IEEE Comput. 44, 51–58.

Tsiftes, N., Dunkels, A., 2011. A database in every sensor. Proceedings of the 9th ACM Conference on Embedded Networked Sensor Systems, pp. 316–332.

Weber, R.H., 2010. Internet of things, new security and privacy challenges. Comput. Law Security Rev. 26, 23–30, January 2010.

Further Reading

Atzori, L., Iera, A., Morabito, G., Nitti, M., 2012. The social internet of things (SIOT) when social networks meet the internet of things: concept, architecture and network characterization. Comput. Networks 56 (16), 3594–3608.

Atzori, L., Iera, A., Morabito, G., 2014. From "smart objects" to "social objects": the next evolutionary step of the internet of things. IEEE Commun. Magaz. 52 (1), 97–105.

Balenson, D., McGrew, D., Sherman, A., February 1999. Key management for large dynamic groups: one-way function trees and amortized initialization. Internet draft.

Ballardie, A., May 1996. Scalable multicast key distribution. RFC 1949.

Bonetto, R., Bui, N., Lakkundi, V., Olivereau, A., Serbanati, A., Rossi, M., 2012. Secure communication for smart IOT objects: protocol stacks, use cases and practical examples. In International Symposium on a World of Wireless, Mobile and Multimedia Networks (WoWMoM), pp. 1–7. IEEE.

Briscoe, B., 1999. Marks: zero side effect multicast key management using arbitrarily revealed key sequences. Networked Group Communication, pp. 301–320.

Challal, Y., Seba, H., 2005. Group key management protocols: a novel taxonomy. Int. J. Informat. Technol. 2 (1), 105–118.

Chiou, G.H., Chen, W.T., 1989. Secure broadcasting using the secure lock. IEEE Transact. Softw. Engineer. 15 (8), 929–934.

Daghighi, B., Kiah, M.L.M., Shamshirband, S., Rehman, M.H.U., 2015. Toward secure group communication in wireless mobile environments: issues, solutions, and challenges. J. Network Comput. Appl. 50, 1–14.

De Meulenaer, G., Gosset, F., Standaert, F.X., Pereira, O., 2008. On the energy cost of communication and cryptography in wireless sensor networks. In IEEE International Conference on Wireless and Mobile Computing, Networking and Communication, pp. 580–585.

Dworkin, M., 2007. Recommendation for block cipher modes of operation: The ccm mode for authentication and confidentiality. SP-800-38c, NIST, US Department of Commerce.

Eschenauer, L., Gligor, V.D., 2002. A key management scheme for distributed sensor networks. Ninth ACM Conference on Computer and Communications Security, pp. 41–47.

Freeman, T., Housley, R., Malpani, A., Cooper, D., Polk, W., 2007. Server-based certificate validation protocol (SCVP). Internet proposed standard RFC, 5055.

Gharout, S., Bouabdallah, A., Challal, Y., Achemlal, M., 2012. Adaptive group key management protocol for wireless communications. J. UCS 18 (6), 874–898.

Granjal, J., Monteiro, E., Sa Silva, J., 2010. Enabling network-layer security on ipv6 wireless sensor networks. Proceedings of IEEE GLOBECOM, 2010.

Gura, N., Patel, A., Wander, A., Elberle, H., Shantz, S.C., 2004. Comparing elliptic curve cryptography and RSA on 8-bit CPUs. Proceedings of the Sixth Workshop on Cryptographic Hardware and Embedded Systems (CHES-04), pp. 119–132.

Harney, H., Muckenhirn, C., July 1997. Group key management protocol (GKMP) architecture. RFC 2093.

Hui, J., Thubert, P., 2011. Compression format for ipv6 datagrams over IEEE 802.15.4-based networks. RFC 6282, IETF, 2011.

Hummen, R., Hiller, J., Henze, M., Wehrle, K., 2013a. Slimfit – a hip dex compression layer for the ip-based internet of things. IEEE WiMob, pp. 259–266.

Hummen, R., Wirtz, H., Ziegeldorf, J.H., Hiller, J., Wehrle, K., 2013b. Tailoring end-to-end IP security protocols to the internet of things. In 21st International Conference on Network Protocols (ICNP), pp. 1–10. IEEE.

Hummen, R., Ziegeldorf, J.H., Shafagh, H., Raza, S., Wehrle, K., 2013c. Towards viable certificate-based authentication for the internet of things. HotWiSec '13 Proceedings of the 2nd ACM Workshop on Hot Topics on Wireless Network Security and Privacy, pp. 37–42.

Kamat, S., Parimi, S., Agrawal, D.P., 2003. Reduction in control overhead for a secure, scalable framework for mobile multicast. IEEE International Conference on Communications, ICC'03, vol. 1, pp. 98–103.

Kerckhoffs, A., 1883. La cryptographie militaire. Journal des Sciences Militaires XI, 161–191.

Kim, Y., Perrig, A., Tsudik, G., 2004. Tree-based group key agreement. ACM Transact. Informat. Syst. Security (TISSEC) 7 (1), 60–96.

Lee, P., Lui, J., Yau, D., 2006. Distributed collaborative key agreement and authentication protocols for dynamic peer groups. IEEE/ACM Transact. Network. 14 (2), 263–276.

Malan, D., Welsh, M., Smith, M., 2004. A public-key infrastructure for key distribution in tiny OS based on elliptic curve cryptography. First Annual IEEE Communications Society Conference on Sensor and Ad hoc Communications and Networks, 2004, pp. 71–80.

Mehdizadeh, A., Hashim, F., Othman, M., 2014. Lightweight decentralized multicast–unicast key management method in wireless ipv6 networks. J. Network Comput. Appl. 42, 59–69.

Montenegro, G., Kushalnagar, N., Hui, J., Culler, D., 2007. Transmission of ipv6 packets over IEEE 802.15.4 networks. RFC 4944, IETF, 2007.

Ortiz, A.M., Hussein, D., Park, S., Han, S.N., Crespi, N., 2014. The cluster between internet of things and social networks: review and research challenges. IEEE Internet of Things J. 1 (3), 206–215.

Piao, Y., Kim, J., Tariq, U., Hong, M., 2013. Polynomial-based key management for secure intra-group and inter-group communication. Comput. Math. Appl. 65 (9), 1300–1309.

Prashar, M., Vashisht, R., 2012. Survey on pre-shared keys in wire-less sensor network. Int. J. Sci. Emerg. Technol. Latest Trends 4 (1), 42–48.

Rafaeli, S., Hutchison, D., June 2002. Hydra: a decentralized group key management. 11th IEEE International WETICE: Enterprise Security Workshop.

Rafaeli, S., Hutchison, D., 2003. A survey of key management for secure group communication. ACM Comput. Surv. (CSUR) 35 (3), 309–329.

Raza, S., Duquennoy, S., Chung, T., Yazar, D., Voigt, T., Roedig, U., 2011. Securing communication in 6LoWPAN with compressed IPSEC. Proceedings of IEEE DCOSS, 2011.

Raza, S., Voigt, T., Jutvik, V., 2012a. Lightweight ikev2: a key management solution for both compressed IPSEC and IEEE 802.15.4 security. IETF/IAB workshop on Smart Object Security.

Raza, S., Trabalza, D., Voigt, T., 2012b. 6LoWPAN compressed DTLS for CoAP. Proceedings of IEEE DCOSS.

Raza, S., Duquennoy, S., Selander, G., 2013. Compression of ipsec AH and ESP headers for constrained environments. Draft-raza-6lowpanipsec-00 (WiP), IETF, 2013.

Rescorla, E., 1999. Diffie-Hellman key agreement method. RFC2631.

Roman, R., Alcaraz, C., Lopez, J., Sklavos, N., 2011b. Key management systems for sensor networks in the context of internet of things. Comput. Electric Engineer. 37, 147–159.

Romdhani, I., Kellil, M., Hong-Yon, L., Bouabdallah, A., Bettahar, H., 2004. IP mobile multicast: challenges and solutions. IEEE Commun. Surv. Tutor. 6 (1), 18–41.

Sahraoui, S., Bilami, A., 2015. Efficient hip-based approach to ensure lightweight end-to-end security in the internet of things. Comput. Networks 91, 26–45.

Saied, Y.B., Olivereau, A., 2012a. D-hip: a distributed key exchange scheme for hip-based internet of things. Proceedings of IEEE WoWMoM, 2012.

Saied, Y.B., Olivereau, A., 2012b. (k, n) threshold distributed key exchange for hip based internet of things. Proceedings of ACM MobiWac, 2012.

Saied, Y.B., Olivereau, A., 2012c. Hip tiny exchange (tex): a distributed key exchange scheme for hip-based internet of things. Proceedings of ComNet, 2012.

Setia, S., Koussih, S., Jajodia, S., Harder, E., 2000. Kronos: a scalable group re-keying approach for secure multicast. Proceedings of IEEE Symposium on Security and Privacy, pp. 215–228.

Shannon, C.E., 1949. Communication theory of secrecy systems. Bell Syst. Tech. J. 28 (4), 656–715.

Shirey, R., 2000. Rfc 2828: Internet security glossary. The Internet Society, p. 13.

Shirey, R., 2007. Rfc 4949: Internet security glossary.

Veltri, L., Cirani, S., Busanelli, S., Ferrari, G., 2013. A novel batch-based group key management protocol applied to the internet of things. Ad Hoc Networks 11 (8), 2724–2737.

Wander, A., Gura, N., Eberle, H., Gupta, V., Shantz, S.C., 2005. Energy analysis of public-key cryptography for wireless sensor networks. In Third IEEE International Conference on Pervasive Computing and Communications. PerCom 2005, pp. 324–328.

Wong, C.K., Gouda, M., Lam, S.S., 2000. Secure group communications using key graphs. IEEE/ACM Transact. Network., 8 (1), 16–30.

Index

Note: Page numbers followed by "*f*" and "*t*" refer to figures and tables, respectively.

Printed in the United States
By Bookmasters